Contents

Acknowledgments

Writing this book was no easy task and it would have been nearly impossible without the help I received from a number of people. First, I want to thank Art Wentworth. His assistance was invaluable. He did a fantastic job detailing motorcycles, locating special bikes for the photo sessions and posing for pictures. His detailing expertise is second only to his avid interest in motorcycling. In addition to his informative input, Art's overall attitude and enthusiasm helped to make this an entertaining and rewarding project.

Along with Art, I would also like to thank the following folks for sharing their detailing secrets and allowing the use of their motorcycles for photo sessions: Squire Tomasie of Squire's Autowerke in Bellevue, Washington, and his 1980 Harley-Davidson XR 750 Flat Tracker, 1986 Honda Special RF 600 D Flat Tracker and 1989 Kawasaki ZX-10 Ninja; Ralph Maughn and his 1984 Yamaha TT 600 K; Dan Mycon of New Look Autobody in Kirkland, Washington, and his 1988 Harley-Davidson Sportster 883 deluxe; Rory Vance and his 1988 Suzuki Katana 1100; Peter Danikas of Eastside Harley-Davidson in Kirkland, Washington, and his 1988 Harley-Davidson Electra Glide; Bill Buckingham of Buckingham BMW in Seattle, Washington, and his 1985 BMW K100RS; Don Perry and his 1980 Honda Gold Wing Interstate; Bill Myers of Bellevue Yamaha in Bellevue, Washington, and his 1988 Yamaha YFM 100 four-wheel ATV and 1989 Yamaha YZ 80; and Wally Shearer and his son Chris and their 1985 Yamaha Y Zinger; Marsha Fuchs and Steve Giblin of Dewey's Cycle in Seattle, Washington, and their 1970 BSA A65.

I am also grateful for the detailing tips received from Steve Jacobs, Nate Shelton of K&N Engineering, Dave Ireland, Mike Johnson, Vince Barbeaux, Gina Buckingham and Dave Williams.

Barney Li, owner of Eagle 1 Industries, was gracious enough to send along a good sampling of Eagle 1 detailing products, and Mel Miller of Meguiar's offered valuable information about Meguiar's polish, wax and assorted detailing supplies. Employees from the West Seattle Branch of Al's Auto Supply in Seattle, Washington, were very helpful in arranging detailing products on their shelves for picture taking, and I thank them for their patience.

Van Nordquist and Kimberly Brown of Photo Graphic Designs in Everett, Washington, did an excellent job of processing numerous rolls of film and printing each photograph, taking extra time to make sure each shot turned out just right.

Finally, thanks go to Tim Parker, Barbara Harold and Greg Field of Motorbooks International. Their advice, support and editorial assistance is much appreciated and respected.

Introduction

The vast majority of motorcycle enthusiasts not only enjoy riding motorcycles, but also derive a certain pleasure out of maintaining their bikes to optimum performance and appearance standards. It is relatively safe to say, I believe, that the percentage of motorcycle owners far and away outnumber the percentage of automobile owners when it comes to the amount of time and effort spent to clean, shine and detail their particular vehicles.

Although most motorcycle riders agree that a clean machine portrays pride in their ride, many do not see eye to eye on the methods, products and techniques used to get motorcycles to pristine condition. They have certain ways of doing things that work for them and refuse to try anything new, for fear that a new method may not work as well or, heaven forbid, damage their pride and joy. I was, however, able to find at least one viewpoint that seemed to be equally shared by all. That was, the mildest cleaning and polishing methods are much preferred over harsh scouring and abrasive shining.

Detailing is a means of getting motorcycles to look their best without the need for complete dismantling and total restoration. The difference between complete detailing and restoration is that the latter requires a lot of work hours and plenty of money for new parts and old part rejuvenation.

Motorcycle detailing can be fun and rewarding. Although this book will show you how to detail your motorcycle like a professional, it is not intended to be a complete manual showing you how to restore vintage machines. Rather, it is a broad collection of detailing tips and techniques that work well for a number of avid motorcycle enthusiasts, racers and dealers. This book was designed and written for the conscientious and enthusiastic owner who likes to take care of his or her motorcycle and keep it looking its best, using proven methods, products and techniques.

Chapter 1

What is detailing?

At first glance, motorcycle cleaning appears to be quick and easy work. Superficial cleaning is indeed simple, while real detailing is time consuming, labor intensive and very rewarding.

Automobiles present detailers with lots of paint to polish, upholstery to shampoo and big engine compartments to degrease. They are large vehicles with lots of places for dirt to accumulate. Motorcycles do not present those types of cleaning chores. They do, however, challenge the detailer with lots of tiny nooks and crannies and a huge surface area that collects dirt, grease, chain lube and road grime after each and every ride.

Motorcycle detailing is a systematic and in-depth cleaning, polishing, waxing and maintenance endeavor.

A complete detail is generally called for only once or twice a year; it depends on your riding fre-

This engine on a 1988 Harley-Davidson Electra Glide presents a detailer with lots of chrome to shine and many tiny, intricate areas to clean. Attention to detail is what makes this engine sparkle.

quency and routes of travel. A thorough cleaning on a monthly basis will keep your bike looking and performing its best, and, the job can be made much easier if you maintain a weekly maintenance schedule.

Detailing basics

Motorcycle detailing is basically a three-step process. The first is cleaning. An entire day can be spent washing the motorcycle from top to bottom, front to back and side to side. Along with a wash mitt, you will be using paintbrushes to reach inside the engine fins and triple clamp, and a toothbrush to remove wax build-up in emblems and light lenses. Motorcycles are intricate vehicles and include more actual surface area than an automobile. Every part of the bike has to be cleaned before it can be polished, waxed or dressed. This will take time, especially when you consider all the nooks and crannies that are exposed to the elements. Virtually every part of a motorcycle is subject to dust, dirt and road film.

The second part consists of polishing, waxing and dressing. All painted surfaces should be waxed. Polishing is necessary only when the paint is scratched or oxidized. Applying polish and wax is difficult in some areas. It takes time and patience. Chrome- and clear-coated wheels should be waxed, and some enthusiasts even like to wax chrome and black chrome exhaust pipes. Wires, vinyl and rubber trim accessories are lightly treated with Armor All or any brand of polypenetrant. However, because of the slippery nature common with such dressings, seriously evaluate its need before applying to seats, foot pedals and handgrips. At that, use the product sparingly and be certain all excess is removed and the remainder thoroughly buffed.

Dan Mycon is the owner of New Look Autobody in Kirkland, Washington. Along with auto body and paint work, he paints motorcycle tanks and assorted parts. He is a Harley-Davidson fan and loves his new Sportster. He refers to the third part of motorcycle detailing as "getting things right," things like license plate frames, hand lever alignment, cable lubrication and tool kit inspection.

License plate frames from dealers are not always the most appropriate for the bike. A black frame with big white letters generally does not blend well with a full-dress Electra Glide sporting a lot of chrome. A simple chrome frame would look much better. The same is true for a sport bike displaying a white frame with black letters mounted

The first step in motorcycle detailing is washing. Art Wentworth has positioned Squire Tomasie's bike in the shade and next to a drain, to take advantage of indirect sunlight and adequate water run-off control. An entire day can be spent just cleaning a motorcycle.

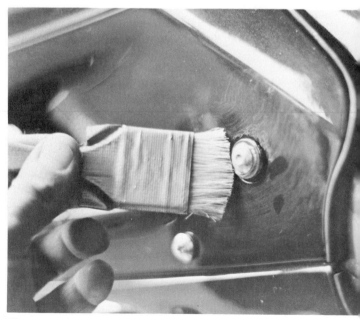

The second part of a motorcycle detail consists of polishing, waxing and dressing. Here, a cut-off paintbrush is used to remove dry polish from around a fairing screw.

on a blue fender with red pinstripes. The gaudy frame draws your eye to it and disrupts the smooth lines of an otherwise sleek road machine. A plain black frame would be more eye appealing.

Motorcycles are symmetrically designed. They have to be in order for riders to maintain balance. It is therefore reasonable to keep a bike evenly proportioned visually. The hand levers should be at the same angle, windshield adjusted squarely and turning signals pointed in the same direction. If you are inclined to apply decals to the windshield, place them in harmony with the front of the bike. One decal on the left side should be mated with one on the right. If only one decal is required (like a parking permit), place it in the middle and square with the bottom edge of the windshield. Let your eye be the judge. If it looks cockeyed to you, it will definitely look worse to someone else.

Tool kits come standard with almost every motorcycle. Although most kits leave a lot to be desired, they can be heaven-sent when a plug fouls or a wire breaks fifty miles from civilization. Take time to clean tools once in a while and make sure they are ready for that unexpected occasion.

Pictures before detailing

All too often, an overzealous detailer will start in-depth dismantling and detailing without contemplating a certain plan of attack or part replacement. He or she will waste time going back over areas already cleaned and may forget how certain parts are put back on the bike. A systematic approach is worthy of consideration.

Motorcycle tool kits are quite handy. They include almost every tool one needs to make emergency repairs in the field or at home. Take care of this tool kit by periodically wiping off the tools and cleaning the vinyl case.

Getting things right is the third part of a detail. License plate frames are sometimes seen as a focal point for the back of a motorcycle. Squire Tomasie couldn't find a suitable frame for the license plate on his bike, and opted instead to mask and paint the outer edge of the plate itself.

This small scratch may have been overlooked during the course of detailing. Photos taken before work starts can be looked at periodically to help a detailer remember particular items that need attention.

9

To help this endeavor, many enthusiasts take pictures of their bikes before starting an annual detail. Some like to use a video camera and take advantage of its audio capabilities to talk about particular areas needing special attention. During the project, they look at photographs and videos to refresh their memory about those special details. When cleaning, polishing, waxing and dressing are complete, they use those pictures again to help them reassemble the motorcycle correctly.

This idea may work well for you. If you don't have a video camera or a camera that produces instant pictures, take photos a week before you plan to detail. This will give the film processor ample time to develop the pictures so you will have them in time for the detail.

Real motorcycle detailing is much more than a wash and wax. Sure, a conscientious wash and wax will make the bike look better, but detailing is what makes the difference between a good-looking bike and one that stands out in a crowd.

Benefits of detailing

A sparkling clean motorcycle is a pleasure to ride. You don't have to worry about soiling new leathers on a dirty seat or staining a pair of white pants stored in the saddlebags. People will admire your new-looking machine and marvel at how many miles are on the odometer.

Personal satisfaction

Touring motorcycles seem to run better when the windshield is clean, sport bikes feel quicker when the engine sparkles and dirt bikes appear to climb better when the knobbies look new. Even though cleaning helps a motorcycle's performance to some degree, most of the improvement is in the rider's mind. When you jump on a dirty bike, you can't help but wonder about its dependability. A detailed bike looks impressive and reliable, and maintains its value.

Personal satisfaction is the very reason you bought your motorcycle in the first place. It is fun to ride with the wind in your face and the sun at your back while enjoying an unobstructed view of the surrounding landscape. Most of us treasure the freedom associated with motorcycling and prefer it to the confines of an automobile. The feeling is tough to explain, but easy to recognize.

Confidence

A well-maintained motorcycle instills confidence in its rider. Dirt riders will climb hills with confidence because they checked all the nuts and bolts, and the chain and sprocket while cleaning the bike after its last ride. The Sunday afternoon enthusiast won't have to worry about breaking down fifty miles from home on his or her sport bike, because all the fluid levels were checked and the bike was serviced after its last weekend trip.

A clean bike looks as if it will run forever, and a detailed motorcycle shows everyone that the rider has pride in his ride. Just looking at a filthy bike, on the other hand, makes one wonder if it will make the five-mile trip to work.

Cleaning the dirt and debris from the engine fins and polishing exposed edges not only helps the top end to run cooler, but also makes the motor look new. Rear wheels collect a multitude of spots from chain lube and the dust that is attracted to it. Cleaning the chain helps to make the entire rear wheel assembly look new. Appearance is important. Like a racer, you can't expect a dirty motorcycle to perform up to its highest standard.

Along with a clean motorcycle, accessories are an important complement. Bug residue on leathers makes them less desirable to wear. Boots with no

Rear wheels collect as much dirt and road residue as any other part of a motorcycle. Attentive cleaning with a small paintbrush helps to clean this area handily.

Squire Tomasie has ridden this Honda Special RF 600 D Flat Tracker at some pretty high speeds. Meticulous and constant attention to service and mechanical performance includes cleaning and detailing after every race.

waterproofing and a scratchy helmet visor can make a short ride feel like an eternity. Motorcycling is supposed to be fun and exciting. Cleaning and detailing for an hour or two after an extended ride, or a few hours on a weekend, will make your bike and accessories look new, feel comfortable and perform as expected.

High resale value

A motorcycle in excellent condition will retain its highest dollar value. Today, some older bikes sell for a lot more money than they did when new. This is because of their rare vintage and immaculate condition.

You can't expect to get top price for a used motorcycle unless it is in top condition. First, of course, it must operate correctly. Second, it has to look as if it has been well cared for and not thrashed around the track or country roads. Removing years of accumulated grease and crud allows the true colors of your motorcycle to shine. Engine, wheels and frame will sparkle, once the layer of road grime is removed.

Most motorcycle enthusiasts, like Art Wentworth, see a dirty motorcycle as an abused

A potential buyer heavily relies upon visual first impressions when considering a motorcycle purchase. Dirt and grease build-up is not only ugly, but also makes one wonder what kind of mechanical service, if any, has been performed on the machine.

Art Wentworth sports full riding leathers, gloves, boots and helmet next to Squire Tomasie's XZ-10.

11

Peter Danikas of Eastside Harley-Davidson will gladly deal on trade-ins. He prefers they be in good overall condition, but is more inclined to accept a clean trade-in needing mechanical work as opposed to a filthy bike that's running fine.

This new motorcycle is suspended next to the window on the showroom floor of Eastside Harley-Davidson. If the lower end of your bike was this clean, how could an interested buyer dispute the machine's value?

motorcycle. If the owner hasn't taken the time to clean the bike, they feel he or she hasn't taken the time to keep up with normal service maintenance. First impressions are always visual and a potential buyer will notice physical imperfections immediately.

Visual impressions are also important to dealers. They prefer trade-ins that will require the least amount of work to make salable and sell fast. A complete detail takes time, and to a dealer, time is money. Peter Danikas is a Harley-Davidson dealer and owns Eastside Harley-Davidson in Kirkland, Washington. He prefers a clean trade-in, even if it needs some mechanical work. Like most dealers, he does not employ someone who just cleans motorcycles. He has to detail the trade himself, or have one of his mechanics do it. With mechanical shop time in the $40 an hour range, it is easy to see that having a mechanic detail motorcycles is not cost-effective.

A day spent cleaning your trade-in will be compensated with a higher trade-in value. Even a quick wash at a self-service car wash will slightly increase the value of your bike. Some extra time spent shining the chrome and polishing the tank will help even more.

If you completely detail your bike before selling, you will be able to point out the cleanliness of the lower end and kickstand area to a potential buyer. The clean condition of these hard-to-reach areas will certainly impress even the most skeptical customer. Along with clean wheels and tires, frame members and the area under the seat, it will be hard for a buyer to dispute the machine's value. The proof is in the pudding and when a bike looks good and runs well, how can anyone argue with top dollar value?

Reveal mechanical problems

It is tough to find the source of an oil leak under an inch of accumulated grease, dirt and grime. It is also difficult to tighten a nut that is covered with yuck. Detailing helps to make mechanical maintenance easier, more pleasurable and efficient. On a clean engine, it is easy to spot a small oil leak. Once located, repairs are made easier by having a clean surface to work on.

Most of us try to avoid touching greasy engine parts. It is tough to get excited about tuning a motorcycle when you know the end result will be filthy clothes, greasy hands and grime-embedded fingernails. On the other hand, checking fluid levels and adjusting the chain doesn't seem like such a chore on a clean bike. The job takes less time, because you can easily see the adjusting mechanisms and you don't have to spend an hour cleaning up after maintenance is performed. Your tools will stay clean and you won't need a bag of shop towels.

Motorcycle racing mechanics always clean their machines before starting repairs. This gives them a complete, comprehensive view of the motor. Obvious defects, such as cracked hoses or frayed wires, are repaired immediately. Further repairs are not hampered by globs of grease, and small O-rings and washers are not lost in the grime.

Easier general upkeep

Motorcycle detailing is definitely easiest when done after every ride; the amount of dirt and road film is minor and a snap to remove. Although some meticulous enthusiasts like Art Wentworth and Wally Shearer do this all the time, it is suffice to say that most riders don't clean their bikes nearly that much. As in everything else, I believe there is a happy medium.

A quality, general upkeep program combines a weekly wash with a monthly spiff and service, and semi-annual complete detail. Cleaning your motorcycle once a week reduces the amount of grease, chain lube and road film that accumulates on the rear wheel, chain guard and the lower portions of the bike. Frequent washing also helps to prevent dirt and grease from baking onto the front of the engine and exhaust pipes.

Using a soft-bristled paintbrush to clean wheels and engine fins is much easier than scrubbing them with an SOS pad. When a motorcycle is correctly maintained, dirt rinses off almost completely with clear water. We have all seen how easily a freshly waxed car comes clean. The layer of wax prevents dirt and road film from firmly attaching to bare paint surfaces. The same maneuver works for motorcycles. Wax on the frame, wheels, forks, shocks and all painted parts protects the surface and makes cleaning quicker and easier.

Final thoughts

The real key to detailing is time, patience and elbow grease. The difference between a quality detail and a mediocre one is the amount of time the detailer takes and the effort exerted toward subtle items. If you don't have time to detail the entire motorcycle, spend the allotted hours on just one part of the bike, making that area look new. Designate another day to complete the rest of the detail.

A full-blown, meticulous detail needs to be done only once or twice a year. Art Wentworth recommends a complete detail at the end of summer and another at the beginning of spring. This, of course, is assuming you have ridden the bike during the winter. In the interim, a weekly and monthly upkeep schedule will help keep the bike looking good year-round.

Expect a complete detail to take at least two days. In some cases, it may take longer. Ralph Maughn took a 2,100 mile cross-country trip from the northern border of Mexico to the southern one, and then back again. His 1984 Yamaha TT 600 K was ridden in dirt, sand, gravel, dry lake beds, pavement, concrete and saltwater. Detailing his bike before the trip took a few weeks and included a lot of disassembly and part replacement. Learning about extended desert trips from magazines, books, other riders and his own past experience helped him prepare his bike correctly and resulted in no major problems throughout the adventure. After recuperating from his lengthy excursion, he took a few weeks to completely detail the bike again.

Dirt bikes, sport machines and touring motorcycles all need periodic detailing. Regardless of the make or model, a complete detail once or twice a year, followed by a weekly and monthly maintenance schedule will help keep your motorcycle looking new, standing tall and remaining valuable.

Washing a motorcycle after every ride is by far the easiest way to maintain its appearance. Dirt and road grime will be fresh, so to speak, and much easier to remove from the wheels, tires, fenders and so forth.

Chapter 2

Tools and materials

From a detailer's standpoint, motorcycles are intricate machines. There are hundreds of tiny, hard-to-reach areas that constantly collect dust, dirt, road grime, oil and grease. It would be nice if there was a miracle spray-on, rinse-off product that would clean these surfaces fast and efficiently. But, as Bill Buckingham says, "There are no miracle products, except of course, elbow grease."

It is the contention of most of the motorcycle enthusiasts I talked to, that harsh chemicals present more of a damage hazard than a work savings. Wheel cleaners, for example, may not hurt the wheel at all, but could cause unwarranted wear on nearby plastic pieces. For that reason, they stay clear of constant caustic cleaner use and rely on mild soaps, soft brushes and patience. If, however, you plan to use a chemical wheel cleaner, be sure it is one designed for the material your wheels are made of.

A small assortment of detailing supplies will help to make the job easier, quicker and safer. A limited array of hand tools will last for years. Chances are, you already have most of them. Soaps, cleaners, polishes and waxes generally last a long time and their cost is minimal. Special equipment, such as a pressure washer, is not necessary, except as a luxury for motocross bikes caked

This is an assortment of cleaning and detailing supplies commonly used by motorcycle enthusiasts. It includes a water supply, wash bucket, wash soap, wash mitt, cleaner, steel wool soap pads, powdered cleanser, dressing, wax, plastic polish, chrome polish, brushes, cotton swabs, towels and touch-up paint.

The best way to clean this part of a motorcycle is with a paintbrush, toothbrush, time and patience. After a thorough wash, it is a good idea to lubricate the hinge point of the brake lever and the linkage attached to it.

with a solid layer of mud from a weekend in the dirt.

Brushes

Brushes are a must for motorcycle detailing. The bristles reach where no towel or cloth ever will. One brush will not be sufficient; I don't know of any brush that is stout enough for tires and yet soft enough for painted parts. You will need an assortment of at least three, while six is preferred.

A plastic-bristled brush is good for tires, seats, foot rubbers and some unpainted frame and engine parts. The rugged bristles are strong enough to dislodge dirt and embedded grime from rubber, vinyl and textured metal surfaces. Used in conjunction with a multi-purpose cleaner, this brush will help make dirt- and grime-encrusted pieces look new.

Supermarkets carry a variety of plastic-bristled brushes. Size and shape are important. A bulky rectangular brush is awkward for tire scrubbing, for instance. You may find a smaller brush equipped with a handle or finger guard more suitable. Before you go brush shopping, determine which parts of your bike will require brush scrub-

Brushes play a significant role in any detail. Auto parts stores and supermarkets carry an assortment of sizes and shapes. More than one design may be needed during your detailing endeavors.

bing and purchase one that will be most versatile in size, shape and manageability. If you decide one brush will not be suitable for all the chores ahead, get a couple of different styles. They are inexpensive and will last a long time.

Most auto parts stores carry an assortment of cleaning, polishing, waxing and dressing supplies. It is tough to recommend one product over another. You will have to experiment with various ones until you come up with a combination that works well for you.

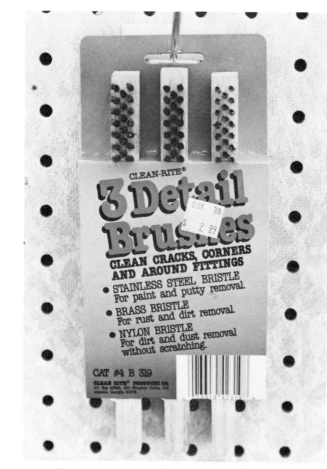

A package of small detail brushes can be found at an auto parts store. About the size of a toothbrush, these brushes work quite well. Use caution with the stainless steel and brass brushes to avoid unnecessary scratches.

Chris Shearer is using a small plastic brush to brighten the knobbies on his bike. This brush has a notch cut out of the base for finger insertion, thus allowing for a solid grip to maintain scrubbing control.

A plastic-bristled brush with a handle is appropriate for tire scrubbing. The handle makes for easy control while scrubbing, and the plastic bristles do not present a scratch hazard to wheels.

This wire brush is made for scrubbing whitewall tires. The wire bristles are short and stout and cropped closely together to brighten whitewalls to their whitest.

An old, soft toothbrush has many uses during a detail. The short bristles and narrow design allow easy access to carburetors, clamp screws, seat beads and lots of other parts. It is a good idea to have two on hand; one for dirty work around the center stand, engine and swing arm, and another for light work on seat beads, spokes and lights.

Toothbrushes work very well to remove wax build-up in the lettering on reflector lenses, the slots of Phillips screws and around the edge of carriage bolts. The soft texture of an old toothbrush may require a longer scrub, but the gentle agitation of soft bristles presents almost no scratch hazard.

Throughout the detail, you will find many uses for a toothbrush. It can be used to clean tools in the factory tool kit, edges around the spark plug cap of ignition wires, nipples on the rim of chrome-spoked wheels, instrument clusters, shift lever rubbers and so on. You can even insert the handle into a towel and use the rigid support to clean between engine fins.

A small, one-inch-wide paintbrush with the bristles cut to about three quarters of an inch, is excellent for removing dried wax in emblems, seams and lettering. The extra-soft bristles will not scratch, yet their close cropping and short stature give them plenty of strength to remove wax from fairing seams, gas cap ridges and mounting screws. This is a handy tool to carry with you while buffing off wax with a soft cloth. Each time you notice a bit of wax in a screw slot or seam, dab and twist the brush until the dried wax is broken loose. Then, wipe away with the cloth.

It is a good idea to wrap duct tape around the metal band of this wax removal brush. Many times,

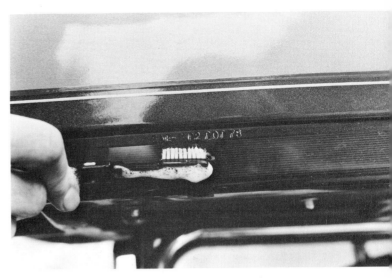

Wax build-up in light lenses is a common detailing oversight. A soft toothbrush makes quick work of removing dried wax and other build-up from lenses and reflectors.

the brush is needed in very tight spaces. Tape will prevent the metal band from scratching or chipping surrounding paint.

Believe it or not, one of the handiest motorcycle washing tools is a paintbrush. Unlike the wax removal paintbrush, these should be left with the long, floppy bristles at full length. Have three sizes on hand for optimum advantage.

A soft, floppy one-inch-wide paintbrush works great for reaching inside spokes to clean axle housings. The narrow size allows easy access into

A paintbrush with the bristles cut to about three quarters of an inch is perfect for removing wax build-up in lettering, emblems and recesses. Note the duct tape wrapped around the metal band on the brush. This is to prevent the band from scratching painted surfaces.

Duct tape should be wrapped around any brush equipped with a metal band. This paintbrush will be used extensively throughout the detail, and tape will prevent accidental scratches on the fuel tank, fairing, fender or any other painted part.

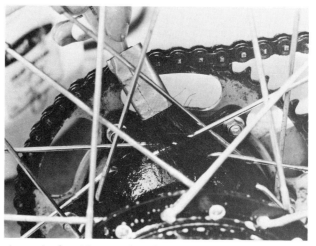

A one-inch-wide paintbrush easily fits into the area of a rear wheel hub to dislodge accumulations of dirt and debris. This size is perfect for reaching into many tight spaces throughout the detail.

Long floppy paintbrushes are excellent tools for washing in tight spaces, such as engine fins. Optimally, a detailer has three sizes available: small, medium and large.

crowded spaces under seats, behind engine heads, inside fairing openings and between triple-clamp assemblies.

The medium, two-inch-wide paintbrush gives you more cleaning power on surfaces that provide larger access, such as instrument clusters, fender edges, headlight assemblies, saddlebag mounts and engine cases. Since it can cover twice the area of a smaller paintbrush, work goes faster with just as much efficiency. Carry brushes in the bucket of wash soap so they are always readily at hand.

A large, four-inch paintbrush works best on wide open areas like the fuel tank, fairing and

The medium-size paintbrush is better suited for cleaning jobs in more open areas, such as the headlight assembly on this Electra Glide. Soft bristles reach inside trim ring pieces to dislodge bug residue and make the part look crisp.

wheel rims. Although not a real necessity, this size is useful for reaching into the long seams on fairings to loosen up bug residue, and along the bottom ridges of fuel tanks to clean off the build-up of road grime and dirt.

Regardless of size, paintbrushes help to clean the tiny grooves, seams and ridges so common on motorcycles. This helps make the machine look crisp. A soft floppy paintbrush is ideal for cleaning inside the groove between the mirror and mirror housing. It can also wipe away dust and dirt between the fins on a head and along the wiring harness. Carried in the wash bucket, you suds up part of the bike with the wash mitt and then follow with the paintbrush for integral pieces. As you continue cleaning, you'll find yourself reaching for the paintbrush time and time again.

Soap

Enthusiasts agree that mild soap is best for washing motorcycles. Seldom will you find a conscientious detailer washing his or her bike with powdered laundry soap. An undissolved granule of soap caught in the wash mitt could scratch paint.

As much as these folks agree on mildness, it is tough to get them to agree on which brand of soap is best. Some prefer liquid dish soap, while others use only name-brand car wash soaps. The difference in opinion seems to focus around the soap's tendency to remove wax. Art Wentworth uses an inexpensive dish soap with good success. He also waxes his bike once a month. Dan Mycon prefers to use name-brand car wash soaps on the basis that these soaps were designed and tested on automotive vehicles, not dishes.

Liquid dish soaps are advertised as mild for hands and tough on grease. A product with degreasing capability is nice, especially when cleaning a rear wheel covered with chain lube. If that soap is supposed to be mild on hands, it should also be gentle on paint and plastic. On the other hand, car wash soaps were designed to clean cars and other motorized vehicles. Engineers tested these products on painted surfaces and planned for them to be easy on wax.

You will have to determine which type of soap to use in your wash bucket. Auto parts stores carry an assortment of car wash soaps like Meguiar's and

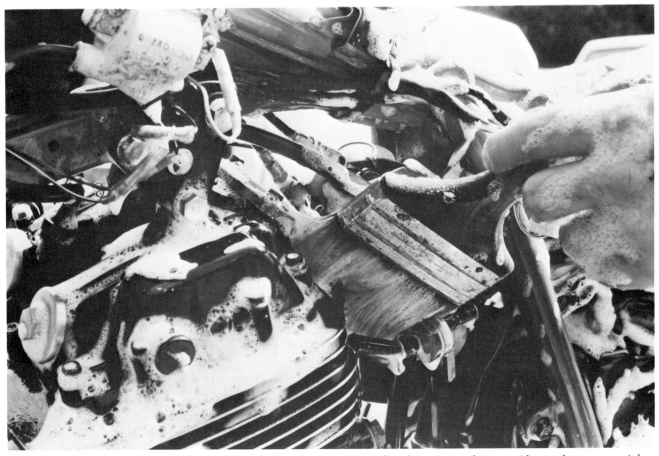

Large paintbrushes make quick work of cleaning wide open areas. Although not used as much as the smaller paintbrushes, it can clean a wider surface area quicker and with just as much intensity.

19

Eagle 1. Turtle Wax and Simoniz also offer good car wash soaps, as does Shur Wonder-Wash. You might consider testing these products, along with liquid dish soaps such as Ivory and Dawn. Sooner or later, you will discover which soap works best for you and your motorcycle.

Peter Danikas has had good luck using S100 motorcycle cleaner. Follow the directions on the label to quickly remove grease and grime from your motorcycle.

Carry a paintbrush in the wash bucket and use it right after sudsing up with the wash mitt. This way, you can take advantage of the suds already in place, as is being done on this rear fender of an Electra Glide.

Enthusiasts disagree as to which wash soap is best. You shouldn't go wrong using any brand of wash soap, as long as the directions on the label are followed. Experiment with a number of them until you find the one that works best for you.

Eagle 1 has a product designed for motorcycle wheels and engines. It can be found at most auto parts stores. Be sure to follow the instructions on the label for optimum results.

20

All-purpose cleaners

Car wash soaps and dish soaps do a fine job of cleaning light surface dirt and road film. But for heavy cleaning around the engine, center stand, wheels and chain, you need a heavy-duty cleaner like Simple Green or S100. Bill Buckingham has had good results using all-purpose cleaners such as 409 and Mr. Clean. Ralph Maughn likes to use Windex with Ammonia-D because it cuts grease and gasoline stains and doesn't streak plastic or chrome. Once again, the choice is up to you.

Simple Green and S100 are designed to cut grease and road oil from automotive vehicles. Consideration was given to the surfaces they come in contact with and what job they are required to do. Squire Tomasie was having a problem with all-purpose cleaners corroding aluminum pieces on his 1986 Honda RF 600 D flat-track special. He tried Simple Green with cold water and liked the results. The cleaner did an excellent job of cutting grease, grime and road oil with no corrosion problems. Equally satisfactory results were found with S100.

Most cleaners come in a variety of sizes and prices. Small squirt-bottle containers are the most expensive. For an economical approach, buy a large container and use it to refill squirt bottles as they empty.

Regardless of the cleaner you use, always read the label completely. Some may contain cautions that could apply to the type of surface you plan to clean. Also, stay abreast of the latest motorcycle cleaner innovations by reading motorcycle consumer magazines reporting on product tests and results.

Wash mitt

Different types of wash mitts are available at auto parts stores and variety stores. Cotton wash mitts are preferred because they don't cause swirls or spider webbing as do some synthetic kinds. Generally, the word chenille will be on the package containing a cotton wash mitt.

The synthetic material used in imitation mitts can cause tiny scratches called spider webbing. These scratches are not visible except in bright sunlight, where it looks as if a hundred spiders crawled all over the gas tank and oil reservoir, leaving behind a maze of webbing. To remove spider webbing, polish with Meguiar's #7 or an equivalent sealer/glaze.

You can use an old towel for motorcycle washing, but a wash mitt works much better. It holds plenty of soap and water and is much more manageable. Try to keep your hand inside the mitt. This will protect your skin against cuts and scratches from sharp objects on the frame and around the engine.

It is a good idea to have two mitts on hand during the washing phase of a full detail. An older mitt

Simple Green is a favorite among many motorcycle enthusiasts. It comes in a variety of sizes, and works well to break loose grease and road film from all parts of a motorcycle.

is used under the bike and along those pieces that collect the most grease and oil. The other mitt is saved for washing those areas that are more likely to be soiled with light surface dirt, such as the fuel tank, seat and windshield.

The thick nap of a cotton (chenille) wash mitt is apt to collect grit. You should rinse the mitt with

Don Perry prefers to buy Simple Green in the large gallon container and uses it to refill a small squirt bottle that he uses for actual application. He likes the handy size of the small squirt bottle, as it can be easily maneuvered in tight spaces around his Gold Wing.

Cotton (chenille) wash mitts are preferred among motorcycle enthusiasts because they do not scratch paint or cause spider webbing as do some synthetic mitts.

clear water regularly in order to remove embedded grit and prevent scratch hazards. Rinse it, for example, after washing the fairing and then again after washing the front wheel assembly. Should the mitt fall on the ground, thoroughly rinse it with clear water from the garden hose. The wash bucket should also be rinsed periodically. Grit tends to collect at the bottom of the bucket and can be picked up by the mitt. It is not uncommon to rinse the bucket and start out with a new soap mix three or four times during a detail.

Drying cloths

Soft cotton towels work best for drying a motorcycle after a thorough wash. Art Wentworth likes to carry two towels when drying. The first absorbs most of the water and the second removes any lingering moisture. Extra-large bath towels are too cumbersome to work with. Use an ordinary cotton hand towel, or, cut a large one in half.

Fold the first towel in quarters. As one side becomes saturated, turn it over to a dry side. The pickup towel works best when folded in half. The thinner size allows better access to tight areas around instruments, triple clamps and the like.

To reach standing water at the base of windshields, engine fins and fairing seams, use paper towels. The absorbent nature of these towels "wick" water out of tight spaces that towels cannot fit into. Paper towels are also useful in removing large globs of grease from the bottom of the engine and along chain guards before washing. When they are full of grease, just throw them away.

Old cotton socks—clean of course—work well for applying polish to odd-shaped pieces like shift

It is a good idea to have two wash mitts available for motorcycle cleaning. One mitt can be used on lower areas commonly covered with grease. A newer mitt should be saved for cleaning painted parts like fairings and fenders.

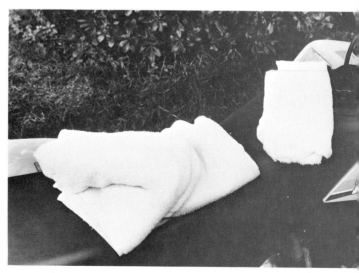

Have a few soft cotton towels available for drying your motorcycle after the wash. As one becomes damp, hang it up and use a fresh one. After detailing, throw them in the washer and dryer to prepare them for the next detail.

levers, exhaust pipes and handlebars. You can easily fit your hand into them, and work the polish into the surface without having a bulk of extra cloth getting in the way. For polishing and waxing spokes, put a sock on one hand to apply and another sock on the other hand to buff.

Old cotton T-shirts and flannel shirts are good for polish and wax removal. The soft material buffs off wax residue from painted pieces with no scratch worries. The problem is, how many old shirts do you have hanging around? Wentworth claims he doesn't own any "old" clothes, so he goes to the yardage store and buys pure white flannel. He cuts the square yard section into pieces a foot square. The small size is perfect for buffing off wax from fuel tanks, fairings and other painted parts. When the cloth becomes impregnated with wax residue, he just puts it into the washing machine and clothes dryer. The cloth comes out clean and soft, ready for the next detail.

Polish, wax and dressing applicators

Polish and wax can be applied with a soft towel, an applicator that came with the product or a small rectangular household sponge. Wentworth prefers the straight edges on a small sponge for polish and wax application on painted motorcycle pieces. It allows him easy application along painted edges next to vinyl seats and rubber pieces. Ralph Maughn uses a piece of an old cotton T-shirt. He likes to use his finger inside the cloth to apply polish and wax in tight areas.

Paper towels serve a number of purposes during a detail. In this instance, a paper towel is used to "wick" water from under a bracket at the base of an engine. At other times, paper towels can be used to remove large globs of grease from under the engine and then just thrown away.

Extra-large bath towels are too cumbersome for motorcycle detailing. Hand towels are a handier size. If a bath towel is all you have, consider cutting it in half.

Cleaning, polishing and waxing spokes is a tiresome chore. Hand towels and cleaning cloths sometimes get caught in the spokes, to make matters worse. Try using a soft cotton sock for those endeavors. It will stay on your hand and will not present a bothersome trailing tail.

Use a very soft cloth to wipe off polish and wax residue. This Honda fuel tank has been waxed and is being buffed with a soft piece of white cotton flannel.

The main concern with a polish or wax applicator is that it be soft and clean. Sponges are good because they can be rinsed and cleaned frequently with just clear water. If the piece of T-shirt becomes impregnated with wax, throw it away and get a new one.

A small towel, about the size of a common washcloth, works best for multi-purpose dressing application. The size is great for applying dressing on small accessories without smudging surrounding areas. Use this cloth for dressing only. Best results are found when dressing is squirted onto the cloth first and then wiped onto rubber or vinyl pieces. Since the cloth will be used for dressing

A small rectangular household sponge works great as a polish and wax applicator. The size is handy and maneuverable, and the straight edges allow excellent control around obstacles.

only, it will stay relatively clean. After a while, it will become saturated with dressing and can be used to touch up minor spots.

Rory Vance seldom applies Armor All or any other polypenetrant to the seat, handgrips or foot rubbers on his 1988 Suzuki Katana 1100. Dressing these parts makes them slippery, which can turn them into major riding hazards. Save dressing for those rubber and vinyl parts that are not part of the rider's operational controls. Such would be vinyl tool kit cases, rubber light fixture mounts, wiring, cables and so forth.

Water applicators

An ordinary garden hose nozzle is usually sufficient for motorcycle cleaning. Generally, there is no compelling reason for the use of high water pressure. Fog spray from a garden hose with normal pressure works well to remove soapsuds, loose dirt and grit residue. Avoid spraying water directly onto gauges, radio speakers and electrical controls. To safely remove soapsuds and dirt from these areas, turn the water pressure down by closing the spigot until you get just a slow-moving dribble out of the end of the nozzle.

On occasion, a pressure washer can make the job of cleaning an unusually dirty motorcycle easier. Although detail work is not performed with a pressure washer, it is used to remove extra-heavy accumulations of dirt and grease in preparation for definitive cleaning. Such would be the case of a dirt bike laden with mud after a day of riding in a semi-dry riverbed, or a neglected used bike ready for its very first detail.

A portable pressure washer can be rented at a rental yard for about $10 a day. Better yet, you can bring your bike to the self-service car wash and use that high-pressure system for less than $2. A dirt bike can be left on the trailer or in the back of a pickup truck for this kind of quick cleaning.

Whenever you use high water pressure on a motorcycle, you must be aware of associated hazards. Water can easily be forced into electrical connections, light fixtures and instrument clusters. Grit may be forced into the chain and damage O-rings. Stickers and decals can be peeled off and paint chips enlarged. Keep the pressure washer wand two to three feet away from the surface you are cleaning; water pressure is reduced as the distance between the end of the wand and the cleaning surface becomes greater. Use the wand judiciously to knock off the big accumulations, saving detail work for your driveway and garden hose low water pressure.

Work area

An ideal motorcycle detailing area would include a large, heated, covered garage with plenty of light, a slop sink with hot and cold water, a workbench for cleaning and painting dismantled parts and a concrete floor equipped with a drain. Most of us do not have such a facility and have to make do with what we have.

Extra-dirty and greasy bikes are preliminarily cleaned at a self-service car wash, where residue is easily washed away into drains designed for such run-off. Detailed cleaning will not produce a great deal of greasy residue and can therefore be completed in your driveway without much worry of staining the paved surface.

Optimally, the wash area should slope away from the bike, preferably into a drain or curb. This will prevent puddles of water forming around the bike and help keep your feet dry. A concrete or paved surface is cleanest and most appropriate. A gravel driveway will work, but causes tires to pick up grit when the bike is moved into the garage for waxing.

It is best to wash bikes in the shade. This is to prevent sunlight from quickly evaporating water droplets and causing water spots. If no shady area is available, and you are forced to wash your motorcycle in the sun, wash the shady side first and then the sunny side. Rinse the bike frequently to prevent soapsuds from drying on the surface, and dry the bike as soon as possible to avoid the formation of water spots.

Work clothes

It may not seem like an important part of motorcycle detailing, but comfortable clothes and shoes make the endeavor more pleasant. Tight-fitting jeans will make constant bending and twisting an unnecessarily tiring chore. Open sandals allow cold water and grit to fall on your feet and between your toes, and a big bulky shirt just gets in the way.

Some detailers like to wear short-sleeved coveralls, others prefer sweat pants and a T-shirt. Tennis shoes are fine during warm weather, while work boots may be better during fall and winter months. In other words, comfort is the key. You will be bending over to reach engine, wheel and frame parts, so wear trousers that stretch with you. Jeans with rivets on the pockets present scratch hazards, as do shirts and jackets with exposed zippers. Be alert to these items and use caution around the fuel tank, fairing and other painted and polished parts.

If you find yourself leaning over the bike to reach particular areas, consider wearing a long apron. This will prevent buttons and belt buckles from scratching the tank or fairing.

All jewelry, rings and watches should be removed before washing, polishing or waxing your motorcycle. Watches and bracelets can easily scratch any painted surface they come in contact with. Rings present a couple of hazards. First, while washing the bike, a ring could catch on a

Care must be given radio and CB speakers while washing a motorcycle. Even though speakers are waterproof, avoid squirting water directly at or into them. Covering speakers with towels while washing the top of a motorcycle provides an added measure of protection.

clamp or screw and may injure your finger. Second, if your hand slipped off of a cleaning cloth or towel, a ring would surely scratch the surface you were wiping.

Soap pads and steel wool

SOS pads, Brillo pads and #00 and finer steel wool are useful detailing tools. They are used to

High-pressure water should be judiciously applied. Forcing water into the steering bearing causes dirt and grit to be forced into the bearing as well. Detailed cleaning cannot be done with a high-pressure water wand, use it to just remove big accumulations of debris.

A good wash area will provide protection from the sun, a slope for water run-off and an adequate water supply.

Concrete is a preferred surface, although pavement and gravel are acceptable.

This bike was washed in sunlight for photo purposes only. Motorcycles should always be washed in the shade. On a warm sunny day, a T-shirt, shorts and ten- nis shoes may be the most comfortable detailing outfit to wear.

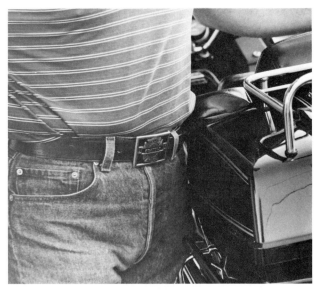

Especially on large touring bikes, be aware of belt buckles and rivets on trousers. These items present a scratch hazard every time you lean over or next to the motorcycle.

A steel wool soap pad is used to brighten the engine fin edge on Squire Tomasie's Flat Tracker. Just a few swipes is all that's needed. It is better to make two or three light passes than to scour once.

scrub whitewall tires, stained bare metal (not polished) engine pieces, chrome exhaust pipes and some plastic dirt-bike fenders and fuel tanks.

Soap pads are soft and make quick work of cleaning dirty carburetors and chrome-spoked wheels. They can even be used on some vinyl

pieces where encrusted dirt won't come off with a toothbrush.

Basically, these pads can be used wherever needed, as long as you realize their scratch potential. Polished alloy and aluminum pieces, and painted parts like fuel tanks and fairings, should not be scrubbed with steel wool soap pads. You must use common sense. These pads tend to fall apart rather easily, so have more than one on hand.

Use #00 and finer steel wool, up to #0000, along with liquid wax to polish chrome. A few en-

Steel wool soap pads are great detailing tools. They can be used to clean bare metal parts and whitewalls. Have more than one available, as they tend to fall apart rather quickly.

Most chemical wheel cleaners are designed for automobile wheels. Some enthusiasts have successfully used them on their motorcycles. Although great for a one-time cleaning of badly neglected wheels, some enthusiasts are concerned about the effects these heavy-duty cleaners may have on other motorcycle pieces. Always read and follow the directions on the label.

Auto parts stores generally carry an ample supply of automotive paints. Although color coded for automobiles, you may be able to find a color that matches your bike, most often black. To get special colors matched, check with an auto body paint and supply store.

Harley-Davidson manufactures touch-up paint for most of their motorcycles. This bottle will be used to touch up the nick on a saddlebag. Attached to the cap is a small brush used for application. Follow the directions on the label for best results.

thusiasts prefer to use extra-fine steel wool with Windex for shining chrome to perfection. The combination of fine steel wool and a liquid base quickly removes caked-on residue and the early formation of rusty pits on chrome.

If you are concerned about the effects steel wool or soap pads will have on a certain part of your motorcycle, try a small application on an inconspicuous spot first. If the results are not up to your standards, or scratching occurs, you will not have damaged an otherwise good piece of equipment.

Wheel cleaners

Eagle 1 manufactures a number of automotive chemical wheel cleaners. Turtle Wax, Meguiar's and others also make similar products. These cleaners are intended for use on automobile wheels, although some motorcyclists have used them successfully on their wheels. Bill Buckingham is concerned about what these types of cleaners and caustic chemicals will do to surrounding painted, plastic and vinyl parts. Unlike an automobile where the wheels are basically isolated, a motorcycle features everything close together. Not only will a wheel and tire be sprayed with wheel cleaner, overspray is almost unavoidable on fenders, chains, forks, brake hubs or calipers, cables and so on.

Art Wentworth is concerned about the effects harsh chemicals will have over the long term. He wonders if very slight traces of acid, caught in the nipples of chrome spokes, will eventually corrode them. He chooses to wash wheels by hand with soap and water. A paintbrush and toothbrush help make cleaning easier and quicker.

This is not to say that a specific wheel cleaner, designed to clean the type of material your wheel is made of, will not work safely and effectively. If the wheels on your bike are terribly dirty and stained, and you feel they need an in-depth cleaning with a chemical wheel cleaner, carefully read the labels on the various wheel cleaners at the auto parts store. The information on these labels will describe the type of material they are designed to clean and will give you specific instructions on how to use them. Make sure you follow the directions on the label to the letter. Ignoring specified time frames and other pertinent directions may result in damage to the wheel and possibly other parts.

Paint

Painted kickstands, frames and skid plates are often punished by road hazards and frequently suffer paint chips, scrapes and scratches. Black parts are painted with a quality gloss or semi-gloss. Spray cans of various colors are readily available at most auto parts stores.

Frames used to be black, making touch-up painting an easy task. Over the years, manufacturers have designed motorcycles with frames of various colors, including silver and orange. To repair chips and scratches on these, you need to purchase the correct color of touch-up paint from the dealer. A wide variety is offered, including touch-up for fairings and saddlebags.

Black-painted exhaust pipes, most common on dirt bikes, are painted with heat-resistant paint. This product is also carried by most auto parts stores and motorcycle shops.

Bright silver paint is handy for touch-up on silver-painted front fork pieces and side cases. If the part is heavily chipped, it may be necessary to remove it for sanding and painting. Other chips and scratches are repaired using a fine artist's paintbrush. Deep-pitted chrome can be cleaned and polished with #00 or finer steel wool. Afterward, a light application of bright silver into the pits will cover dark blemishes and will be hardly noticeable.

Paint offers its best coverage and flow when it is warmed to at least room temperature. Small bottles of touch-up and cans of spray paint should be allowed to warm up before application. Although not necessary during warm summer months, they can be heated in a sink of warm water to thin the paint and activate all the potential of the propellent in spray cans. Warnings on the labels of spray paint cans advise against subjecting the contents to

Heat-resistant paint is required on exhaust pipes and most painted engines. Unlike this paint, ordinary enamel or lacquer paint will not stand up to extreme temperatures. Auto parts stores and some motorcycle shops carry an assortment of colors and brands.

temperatures exceeding 120 degrees Fahrenheit. Thus the warm water in the sink should not be too hot for your hand, a temperature far below 120 degrees. Warming the paint to seventy or eighty degrees is sufficient, as paint flows much better at those temperatures than at fifty or sixty degrees.

Multi-purpose dressings

Armor All is a popular product used to rejuvenate weathered vinyl and rubber. Used sparingly, and according to the directions, this type of dressing can make neglected parts look new. Art

This is a small sampling of rubber and vinyl dressings. All of them work well, although enthusiasts have mixed feelings on their use. Try them all until you find one that works best for you.

In extreme cases, tires will not come clean and will require a coat of tire black. This product is a type of paint that is applied to tires to make them look new. After it has been applied, periodic touch-up will be needed to keep tires looking good.

Wentworth uses Armor All exclusively. Dan Mycon refuses to use any kind of polypenetrant whatsoever. He prefers to keep his 1988 Harley-Davidson Sportster clean and protected with a cotton motorcycle cover from Beverly Hills Motoring Accessories. Squire Tomasie likes Meguiar's #40. Once again, you will have to determine which specific product works best for you. Try them all until you discover the one that does the best job for your dressing needs.

As mentioned previously, slippery seats, handgrips and foot rubbers make a motorcycle less safe to operate. Although these parts can be dressed once or twice a year, it is recommended that they stay relatively dressing-free. Other parts can be safely dressed with good results, however.

Tire sidewalls look new after a thorough cleaning and light application of dressing. Stay away from the tread, though, and dress only the sidewall. It is possible to dress too much of the tire, which could cause it to slip while going through a corner.

Rubber light mounts, vinyl saddlebags, tool kits, wires, hoses, vinyl instrument clusters, and cables are carefully dressed for a much improved appearance. Careful attention to detail is important. Dressing looks good on vinyl and rubber but terrible when smudged on paint and chrome.

Meguiar's manufactures a number of cosmetic car care products suitable for use on motorcycles. To polish paint to perfection, read the informative labels on the products to determine which one is best suited for your needs. Auto parts stores carry a good assortment of these products, and auto body paint and supply stores carry an even greater supply.

Polish

Polish is a product designed to shine metal or painted surfaces. Automotive paint polish is also called glaze or sealer. Meguiar's manufactures a very good selection of polish, sealers and glazes. Designed to remove various degrees of oxidation, scratches and spider webbing, each of the Meguiar's products carries a detailed label describing the intended use for the polish inside. You must carefully read the label to correctly choose the polish, sealer or glaze you need. Auto parts stores and motorcycle shops usually carry a good assortment of these products. Since their shelf space is limited, you probably will have to go to an auto body paint and supply store to find all of Meguiar's products displayed.

Rubbing compound is the most abrasive polish made. It is so abrasive, that using it can create more problems than remedies. I doubt you will ever need to use rubbing compound, even for severe paint oxidation problems. Paint is only so thick, and when oxidation has occurred, layers of paint are dead, making the overall thickness of good paint even less. A vigorous polishing with rubbing compound may remove paint right down to the primer.

Meguiar's also manufactures a product called Cycle Cleaner Wax. It is designed for motorcycle paint and fiberglass parts, and will retard rust and corrosion on mag and aluminum pieces. You'll find this product at most motorcycle shops and some auto parts stores.

This is a definitive label on the back of a jug of Meguiar's Mirror Glaze #7. Note that this label states #7 is to be applied to a non-oxidized surface, meaning that it is a fine polish intended to remove very slight spider webbing and dullness, not heavy oxidation.

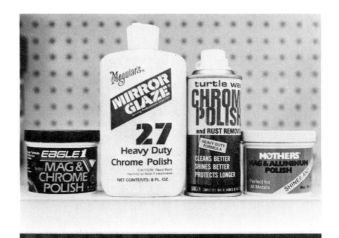

Mag and chrome polishes are available at auto parts stores. Used as directed, they make quick work of shining dull chrome and mag pieces. Enthusiasts have their favorite brands, and, once again, you'll have to try them all to find just the right one for your needs.

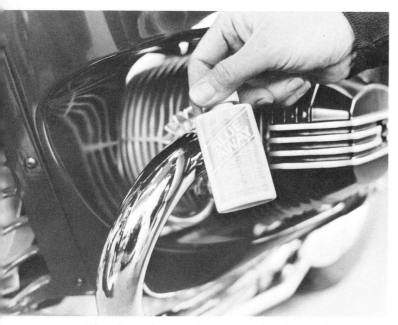

Blue Away is a product especially designed to remove blue blemishes from chrome exhaust pipes. Bill Buckingham used it successfully to clean and shine the chrome exhaust pipe on his vintage BMW.

compound. Follow with an application of sealer/glaze for a deep, lustrous shine.

Eagle 1, Simoniz and Turtle Wax all manufacture various polishes. It is safe to say that most of the products work well for their intended applications. Choosing just the right brand is not always easy, though. I recommend you read labels and talk to fellow motorcycle enthusiasts, detailers and painters to see which products work best for them. Then, try a few yourself until you find the right one for your needs.

Happich Simichrome Polish is a preferred product for most chrome motorcycle parts. It is not necessary to use chrome polish every time you clean your bike. Remember, every polish is somewhat abrasive and removes a minute amount of material each time it is used. Always start a cleaning project with the mildest available method. If a chrome saddlebag mount is dirty, use soap or Simple Green first. If the part is still stained after that, try a chrome polish like Simichrome.

Other polishes are available as well. Harley-Davidson shop owner Peter Danikas likes Mother's, and Bill Buckingham carries Blue Away in his BMW shop for removing the blue stains common on chrome exhaust pipes. Eagle 1 Mag & Chrome Polish works well, and Meguiar's Heavy Duty Chrome Polish #27 is designed for use on badly abused and neglected chrome surfaces.

Wax

There is some confusion over the difference between polish and wax. Primarily, polish shines and wax protects. Polishing compound will shine oxidized paint to look new, but the paint won't stay that way unless it is protected by a thin coat of wax. Carnauba wax is an excellent wax for use on automotive paint surfaces. It offers long-lasting protection against the sun's ultraviolet rays, road hazards

Polishing compound is not nearly as abrasive as rubbing compound. It is much safer to apply polishing compound two or more times than to start out using rubbing compound. Again, you must consider what paint problems you are attempting to remedy. Polishing compound would not be appropriate for light swirl removal, for example. Meguiar's Professional Sealer & Reseal Glaze #7 is better suited for that job. On the other hand, a fuel tank or fairing exhibiting heavy water spots and deep oxidation is a good candidate for polishing

Carnauba-based waxes offer the longest lasting protection. Mother's, Meguiar's and Eagle 1 all manufacture fine carnauba-based products. Wax by itself will not shine. It is to be applied to an already polished surface to keep it looking good and protected from sun rays and the elements.

and the elements. Conversely, wax will not shine. Applied to an oxidized surface, wax will turn white and make the paint look worse.

Many paint care product manufacturers offer one-step cleaner waxes. There are basically two kinds. One type includes some cutting agents for polishing and some wax additives for paint protection and shine longevity. The other type uses solvents and silicones to achieve the same outcome.

Art Wentworth uses Meguiar's Car Cleaner Wax exclusively and refuses to try anything else. He cleans his 1985 Suzuki GS 1150 E sport bike after every ride and waxes it at least once a month. It always looks new and crisp. Dan Mycon believes in carnauba wax. He prefers to use a light Meguiar's polish, like #7, to remove swirls and light blemishes on his Sportster, and then protects paint with a light coat of carnauba wax, such as Mother's. The wax protection on Mycon's Sportster will outlast the one-step cleaner wax on Wentworth's Suzuki. The trade-off is in the application. Wentworth waxes once a month, Mycon waxes every three months.

Eagle 1 manufactures sealer/glazes and carnauba wax, as does Mother's, Turtle Wax and Simoniz. Many other brands are offered as well. Most of them do a fine job and it is almost impossible to recommend one over the other. Meguiar's does offer the widest selection, however.

Unless you have a wax that works well for you, I recommend you talk with other motorcycle enthusiasts and try a number of waxes until you find just the right brand for your needs. If you already have a favorite, why change?

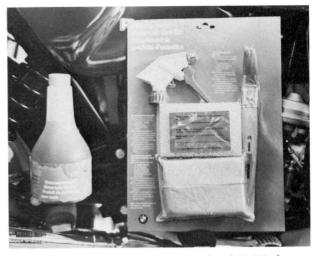

Perched on a vintage BMW is a bottle of BMW cleaner which is similar to S100 and Simple Green. Next to it is a package containing a brush, sponge, chamois-covered pad and a nozzle for the cleaner bottle, also put out by BMW.

Special products

Most of the cleaning tools and supplies you need are available at auto parts stores and supermarkets. Motorcycle shops generally don't carry much of an assortment of cleaning, polishing and waxing products. BMW offers a liquid cleaner similar to S100, and an accompanying kit that contains a squirt applicator for the bottle, a lightweight brush, a sponge and a chamois-covered pad. BMW

This is a great combination for an oxidized and neglected painted tank, fender or fairing. Two applications of polishing compound, followed by two with sealer/glaze will make the surface smooth, rich and blemish-free. A light coat or two of carnauba wax will protect the shine for months.

BMW manufactures a fine and rather unique helmet design. With every new helmet, the purchaser receives a small bottle of helmet cleaner. It is a perfect size to carry on road trips for removing bug splatter and other airborne debris from your helmet.

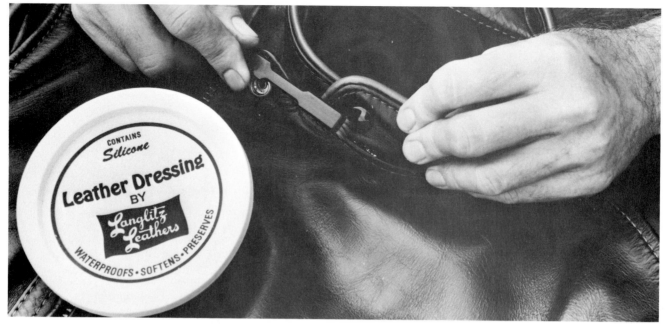

To be on the safe side, always condition leather riding accessories with the products recommended by the manufacturer. This Langlitz coat has a small amount of bug residue next to the collar. A soft toothbrush is used to remove it. After that, a light coat of Langlitz Leather Dressing is applied to rejuvenate the scrubbed area.

Harley-Davidson makes its own brand of chain lube, vinyl dressing and paint. I suggest that Harley owners use these products, since they were developed for this breed of bike.

also offers a small vial of helmet and visor cleaner with every new helmet.

Dave Williams is an avid BMW rider and his BMW R90S looks as if it just came off the showroom floor. He uses Pledge Furniture Polish on his helmet and visor. He says it makes that accessory look good and helps the visor to shed rainwater quickly. Art Wentworth uses Meguiar's Car Cleaner Wax on his helmet and visor with excellent results.

Leather riding gear and boots should be cleaned and conditioned with products recommended by the manufacturer of the equipment. More on these accessories in Chapter 11.

Chain care is an ongoing service item and should be attended to every time you wash your motorcycle, providing yours is equipped with a chain. Harley-Davidson offers its own brand of chain lube, and I recommend Harley owners use it. Wally Shearer uses WD-40 on his dirt bikes. He sprays it on after every ride and boasts that he has never suffered a chain failure. Ralph Maughn applied Lith-Ease white lithium grease to the chain on his 1984 Yamaha TT 600 K every 100 miles during his extensive 2,100 mile Baja, California, trip. He likes it because it does not attract dirt. At the end of the venture, the chain was in good shape and the sprockets looked unused.

Regardless of the chain lube product you use, it is imperative you apply it according to the manu-

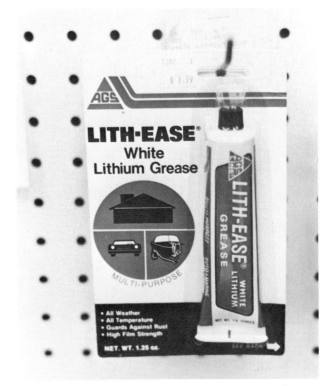

Ralph Maughn has had excellent results using Lith-Ease white lithium grease on the chains of his motorcycles. He says it doesn't attract dust and dirt as do some other chain lubes, and that it lasts quite a while.

After a solid and thorough wash, it is a good idea to lubricate hinge joints on seats and linkages, as well as rear fenders, like this one on a vintage BMW R69S. Art

Wentworth and Wally Shearer like WD-40. You can use your favorite lubricant or the one specified in the owners manual.

facturer's recommendations. Thorough cleaning removes much of the lubricating features of chain lube, as well as lubrication for cables and seat hinges.

Greasy engines and center stand areas sometimes defy the cleaning efforts of Simple Green and S100. For those tough-to-clean areas try Gunk, kerosene or regular solvent. Gunk in the spray can is easy to use, and the solid-stream spray reaches deep into engine crevices. It can also be purchased in gallon containers and then applied through a squirt bottle. The same is true for kerosene and solvent. You will need a heavy-duty squirt bottle, as these powerful petroleum cleaners are hard on seals in the applicator nozzles. When using solvents, be aware that they can cause damage to asphalt pavement by dissolving tar and loosening gravel.

Extra-dirty and greasy engines may require the strength of an engine cleaner for cleaning. Gunk has been successfully used by a lot of enthusiasts. For stubborn tar problems, try Gunk Tar and Bug Remover. As always, be sure to follow the directions on the label.

Chapter 3

Initial wash

Washing a motorcycle correctly entails more than a quick wipe and rinse. It can easily take an entire day to thoroughly clean a bike from top to bottom and side to side. Washing includes much more than just the fuel and oil tanks, wheels, tires and fairing. All nooks and crannies need to be cleaned, including spaces under the seat and engine.

A detailed washing starts from the bottom of the motorcycle and works up. This is so you will stay dry while lying on your back and reaching up to wash the center stand area, skid plate and lower engine parts. After that, efforts are concentrated on various factions of the bike. For example, wash the front wheel and surrounding assemblies before

At the beginning of a wash, while the ground is dry, the lower section of this Sportster is sprayed with Simple *Green and then washed with suds from the wash bucket. A wash mitt and paintbrush work well.*

moving on to the rear wheel and its unique accessories. Clean both sides of each area before moving on.

A motorcycle may be divided into several separate areas for cleaning.

1. Undercarriage:
   a. Exhaust pipes
   b. Center and side stands
   c. Skid plate
   d. Lower engine areas
   e. Shift and rear brake levers
   f. Frame members
   g. Footpegs and rubbers
2. Front wheel:
   a. Tire
   b. Rim
   c. Spokes
   d. Axle hub
   e. Brake assembly
   f. Fender
   g. Forks
   h. Headlight
   i. Cables
3. Rear wheel:
   a. Tire
   b. Rim
   c. Spokes
   d. Axle hub
   e. Brake assembly
   f. Cables
   g. Swing arm
   h. Fender
   i. Taillight
   j. License plate and space underneath
   k. Shock absorbers
   l. Chain, chain guard and sprocket

4. Sides, left and right:
   a. Engine, cylinder head
   b. Carburetor
   c. Wiring
   d. Air cleaner housing
   e. Raised exhaust pipes
   f. Oil tank
   g. Top of engine cases
   h. Linkages
   i. Frame
   j. Lower fairing
5. Top:
   a. Fuel tank (remove tank to clean underneath)
   b. Seat and buddy seat (remove to clean underneath)
   c. Windshield
   d. Fairing
   e. Triple-clamp area
   f. Instrument cluster
   g. Handlebars and grips
   h. Levers and hand controls
   i. Mirrors
   j. Turning indicator lights
6. Extras:
   a. Saddlebags
   b. Tool kit
   c. Intricate emblems and insignias

Washing these areas as separate units allows for convenience and attention to detail. Your cleaning tools and supplies will be close at hand and you will be able to concentrate your efforts on one small space at a time. Before you can expect to get on with the detail, your motorcycle must be as clean as possible. Paint will not adhere to dirty surfaces, and dressing looks terrible when applied over stains.

Pressure washing

Self-serve car wash facilities offer high-pressure water applicators with soap mix and clear

The front wheel of Ralph Maughn's Yamaha requires application of a cleaner and then scrubbing with a paintbrush and toothbrush to remove dirt accumulations on the hub and at the odometer connection.

This tidy Harley-Davidson rear wheel is complemented by a clean valve stem assembly, weights, rim and tire.

A quick run through the self-serve car wash would remove a lot of this dirt accumulation. Detailed cleaning on this side of the engine will have to be equaled by the same cleaning on the other side.

A paintbrush will reach deep inside this handlebar area to remove dirt and dust. Later on, judicious painting with appropriate masking will touch up the lever and make it look new.

water. Generally, stalls are covered and equipped with sufficient drains. For a nominal cost, you can take advantage of this system to remove large concentrations of mud, dirt and grease.

For those bikes suffering problems of grease build-up, you should apply a degreaser, such as

Gunk, kerosene or solvent, before pressure washing. Solvent will start dissolving grease and make the pressure washer more efficient.

Caution: Do not squirt water on a hot engine. Unlike an automobile engine which is mostly made of heavy metal, motorcycle engines are lightweight. Applying cold water to a heated engine

Light applications of engine degreasers, such as Gunk, help to loosen greasy residue to make cleaning easier and more efficient. Use solvents sparingly and be aware that these petroleum-based products can damage asphalt surfaces.

High-pressure water forced into the swing arm joint on this Yamaha could force dirt and grit into the needle bearings. Keep high-pressure nozzles away from bearings and use them only to remove heavy accumulations of mud and dirt.

may cause fractures, warps or other serious damage. Squire Tomasie believes that steam, caused when water is applied to a hot engine, finds its way into the head and begins a rusting process. He always washes motorcycles when the engines are cold.

To take full advantage of high water pressure, the application wand has to be held relatively close to the surface being cleaned. This is fine, as long as the surface will not suffer damage from the pressure. For example, rinsing the engine case at close range should not damage the metal. Using that

same pressure directly on instruments, however, may force water into the gauges. This could result in a fogged lens, rusty gauge face or other problems associated with a moisture-laden instrument.

To avoid unnecessary damage, controlled application of the pressure wand is necessary throughout the wash. Hold the wand away from delicate surfaces like painted fuel tanks and wiring connections. Start rinsing with the nozzle about three feet from the bike. As you deem necessary, move the nozzle closer to remove stubborn grease accumulations. If you notice decals or stickers beginning to peel off, remove the wand immediately. The same is true for flaking paint chips and loose pinstripes.

As stated previously, you cannot detail a motorcycle with a pressure washer. Use it only to remove the big accumulations of dirt and grime and save detailed cleaning for your driveway.

As opposed to hand washing, start pressure washing from the top and work down. This does not mean you should pressure wash a clean fairing and instrument panel before getting to a grease-covered engine case. If the only part in need of the power from a pressure washer is the engine, then just do it. On the other hand, if your dirt bike has globs of mud from the top of the handlebars down to the kickstand and from the front tire to the rear, start at the handlebars and work down to the engine. Then, work on the front wheel area and gradually clean your way to the rear wheel. Wash at a downward angle to prevent splashing mud and grit onto areas previously rinsed.

Be alert to the hazard of water ricochet. Aim the wand at an angle away from your face, and be

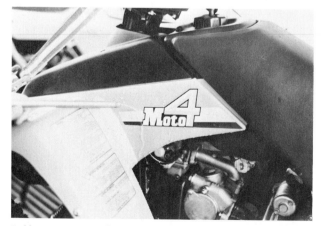

Self-serve car wash systems work well but can also damage those parts not made to withstand high pressure. The decal on this Yamaha four wheeler could be peeled away by high water pressure. There is no need to hold the wand this close to an emblem or decal.

The steering knuckle on the front end of this Yamaha four-wheel ATV vehicle is susceptible to dirt and grease build-up. However, applying high-pressure water through the wand at this close range will force debris into the bearings and may cause undue and premature wear. Hold the wand away from the surface and save detailed cleaning for paintbrushes and toothbrushes.

on guard for water splashing into your eyes. You may consider wearing safety goggles or, at least, sunglasses.

Dirt bikes can be left on their trailer or in back of a pickup truck for this type of quick cleaning. Park a trailer directly over the drain for good results. Park your vehicle so that the open tailgate is over the drain. This way, you'll take advantage of any slope, allowing water to run out of the truck bed and into the drain.

Hand washing
Undercarriage

Basic cleaning of a relatively clean motorcycle is done in a driveway without much worry of staining pavement. With a dry surface to lie on, spray the undercarriage with S100, Simple Green or other heavy-duty cleaner. This product should immediately start to dissolve road grime, dirt and grease.

While the cleaner is still on the bike, use an older wash mitt full of suds to wash under the engine. The center stand mechanism, skid plate and frame should also be washed at this time. When you feel the wash mitt has done all it can do, dip a paintbrush into the wash bucket and fill it with foam. Briskly agitate the paintbrush over all exposed areas. It will dislodge dirt build-up along grooves, around nuts and bolts and next to ridges. Dip the brush into the wash bucket to bring out more foam as needed. Extra-stubborn build-up may have to be scrubbed with the plastic-bristled brush, toothbrush or an SOS pad.

Simple Green is applied to an Electra Glide engine. This cleaner will immediately start to dissolve and loosen dirt and road grime. Follow this with a wash mitt and paintbrush for definitive cleaning.

Rinsing off dirt bikes and other off-road vehicles can be done quickly at a self-serve car wash. Since this will be a light cleaning intended only to remove the big stuff, you can leave the bike in the back of your pickup. Park with the tailgate over the drain to take advantage of the slope so that the bed of the pickup can be rinsed too.

Along with the front of the engine, frame members and skid plate assemblies should be washed while you are lying on the ground and reaching up. This is what the front of Ralph Maughn's bike looked like upon his return from the Baja.

41

A paintbrush is a wonderful detailing tool. Here, it is used to clean the lower side area of a Sportster engine.

Exhaust build-up is a common item at this spot and a paintbrush works well to remove the accumulation.

After the lower section of the bike has been cleaned, the ground will be wet. To keep your pants dry while working on other lower sections, kneel on the garden hose.

When you feel the area has been sufficiently scrubbed, rinse with plenty of clear water. Since your work surface is now wet, kneel on the garden hose to keep your pants dry while bending down to check your work. Heavily soiled spots should be cleaned again. If this additional cleaning requires you to lie on the ground again, move the bike to a dry spot elsewhere on the driveway.

Attention should be given not only to the bottom of the engine, but also to the hinge points of center and side stands. Lubrication fittings and hinge points are almost always covered with grease. The springs that retract these pieces are notorious for collecting dirt, grease and grime. Use the paintbrush or toothbrush to clean the grooves surrounding them. Virtually every part of the bottom of the motorcycle should be cleaned. Concentrate on the lower engine area and the parts around it.

This is also a good time to check for missing nuts, bolts, screws and cotter pins. Repairs or replacement are made later, during detailed cleaning and servicing.

Rinse again with plenty of clear water and check your work. Look closely around bolts and along ridges. Grease and road film build up around the edges of bolts and ridges quite readily. Use a toothbrush with Simple Green to remove them.

The bottom sides of low-mounted exhaust pipes are also cleaned during this phase. Tough, baked-on spots of road oil and dirt may have to be lightly scrubbed with an SOS pad. Art Wentworth has successfully used these pads to clean chrome pipes and even the tips of stainless BMW pipes with no scratch problems. Painted pipes may not fare as well, and you may have to touch them up later with the correct color of heat-resistant paint. Remove build-up from around clamps and screws with a toothbrush.

Footpegs, shift and brake levers, skid plates and frame members also must be cleaned. Bare metal parts are scrubbed with an SOS pad to remove stubborn spots. A toothbrush is used on painted frame and skid plate parts, as well as the rubbers on footpegs and the shift lever.

If globules of grease have fallen off the bike, take a few minutes to remove them. Plain grease is picked up with a paper towel or rag. Then use solvent on a rag to wipe off residue. Other types of non-greasy residue that has accumulated on the ground is washed down the drain with a garden hose. A few minutes spent cleaning this mess prevents you from walking in it and tracking it all over the place while you wash the rest of the bike.

Front assembly

Before you start to wash another area of your motorcycle, check the wash bucket. You may find the water rather dirty and the suds dissolved. If this is the case, rinse the bucket, wash mitt and brushes, and make up a fresh solution of wash soap. The rest of the motorcycle will include

This part of Dan Mycon's Sportster seems to always be covered with exhaust residue. He must maintain a frequent washing schedule to keep this part looking good. A good coat of wax will help to protect it against harsh and corrosive exhaust vapors.

The plastic-bristled brush works well to clean this Electra Glide footrest. A toothbrush may be best suited for reaching inside the narrow grooves on the brake pedal.

While cleaning the lower portions of your bike, take note of missing bolts, screws and nuts. Plan to replace them later, during or right after detailed cleaning.

Vigorous scrubbing with the plastic brush may result in the brush knocking against a painted part, causing a paint chip. Art Wentworth thought it would be a good

idea to hold a wash mitt next to painted pieces to protect them from accidental damage from the brush. The idea works quite well.

Front wheel assemblies are subjected to a lot of road hazards and debris. A light application of cleaner helps to loosen build-up and allows the wash mitt and paint-brush better cleaning ability.

painted pieces, and you should not take the chance of washing them with dirty water and tools.

Other than washing the bottom of the bike first, to stay as dry as possible, the order in which you continue is not critical. Some enthusiasts like to start at the top. They feel that lower sections will trap dirty residue, and by cleaning them last they essentially save a step. Others realize that lower sections of a motorcycle become much more soiled than higher ones. They like to clean the dirtiest items first and then move on to the light stuff. The choice is yours. The most important thing to remember is thoroughness. Stick to a systematic cleaning plan in order to achieve maximum results with the least amount of effort.

Washing front and rear wheels is easiest when the bike is securely placed on its center stand. This enables you to rotate the front and rear wheels without having to move the entire machine. Harley-Davidsons, and others equipped with only a side stand, will have to be moved forward and backward in order to gain access to all parts of the wheel and tire.

Front wheels pick up road oil, dirt and brake dust. Spray the wheel, brake assembly, axle hub and tire with S100, Simple Green or other heavy-duty cleaner first, just as you did on the bottom of the engine. You will see dirt residue start to loosen up right away.

Dip a clean wash mitt into the wash bucket and wash the rim and spokes. Place your hand fully inside the mitt to protect your fingers against cuts and scrapes from sharp edges on spoke nipples. Maneuver your fingers around the wheel, cleaning between spokes and the valve stem. Firmly grasp a part of the rim and tire to rotate the wheel, allowing access to all parts of it. Motocross bikes display front wheels that are clearly open for washing. You may not have to rotate them. Road bikes, however, are usually equipped with large front fenders and fairing pieces that make half of the wheel totally inaccessible. These wheels will have to be rotated for thorough cleaning.

With a good soapy mix on the wheel, use a floppy paintbrush to clean tight spaces missed by the mitt. After that, use the plastic-bristled brush to scrub the tire. Soap up the entire tire, including tread. Look for telltale bubbles denoting an air leak from the tire or tube. Whitewalls are scrubbed with a whitewall brush or SOS pad. Rinse with clear water.

It is a good idea to check your work after rinsing. Missed areas are easier to catch while you are

A paintbrush works great for removing dirt and dust from the slots on brake assemblies. Work the brush into tight spaces with plenty of foam from the wash bucket.

still involved with a particular spot. Slight stains and build-up in spoke nipples are removed with a toothbrush. With the wash mitt on your hand, pinch individual spokes between your fingers for cleaning. Use an SOS pad as needed for stubborn stains. Also check for loose spokes. They can be marked with a piece of masking tape and tightened later.

Spray the axle hub again with Simple Green. Use a small paintbrush to scrub the center of the hub, inside the spokes. The toothbrush is handy to scrub away hardened dirt build-up on the hub center and around spoke attachment points. Rotate the

The design of Squire Tomasie's ZX-10 prevents access to the entire front wheel in one shot. The wheel has to be rotated to achieve total cleaning. On the center stand, it is easy to spin the front tire. If you have a helper available, have him or her push down on the back of the bike to take residual weight off the front, allowing the front tire to spin easier.

Always rinse with plenty of clear water to be sure all of the soapsuds are removed from tiny cracks and crevices. After rinsing, take a moment to inspect your work. Go over areas again that were missed or not cleaned to your satisfaction.

45

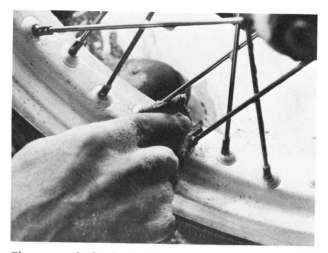

Chrome-spoked wheels can withstand light cleaning with a steel wool soap pad. Do not use these pads on clear-coated wheels, though, as they will mar the clear-coat finish. In this instance, a soap pad is used to remove caked-on build-up at the nipples of a spoked wheel.

Intricate ridges and recesses on front brake assemblies may require the use of a toothbrush for complete cleaning. Spray the area with cleaner, and then bring in a toothbrush full of foam from the wash bucket for super cleaning results.

wheel as necessary to maintain total coverage. You will have to have patience working in this area, especially when the wheel is a chrome-spoked model. Mag-type wheels present no such access problems. They are readily accessible and much easier to clean.

Next is the brake assembly and lower forks. After spraying with cleaner, use a paintbrush and toothbrush to thoroughly clean the mechanism.

Look for build-up at the base of fittings, hoses and cables. Residue in slots and holes on the rotor are washed away with a paintbrush. A toothbrush may be required to adequately clean exposed threaded bolts at the bottom of the forks. Don't forget to wash retainer loops and other accessories that are attached to the lower forks. Use the wash mitt, paintbrush and toothbrush as necessary.

By now, the entire wheel, hub, brake assembly and lower forks should be clean and thoroughly

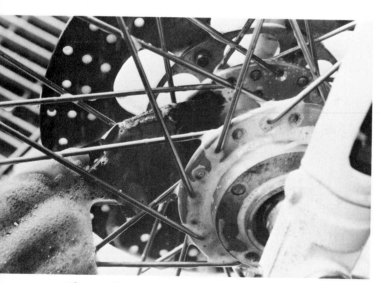

The small paintbrush easily fits into the front wheel hub area for cleaning. Agitate the bristles around the connection point for the spokes to remove dirt and dust build-up. Use lots of foam from the wash bucket and don't be afraid to spray cleaner on that area to help loosen stubborn build-up.

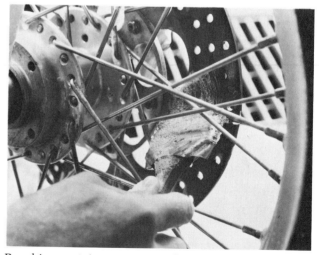

Reaching certain spots around the front wheel is difficult. Use your imagination and ingenuity to come up with ways to adequately clean the area. Reaching through the spokes is an inventive way to clean the inside face of this brake piece with a paintbrush.

rinsed. Work your way up the forks to the fender. Check the condition of the wash mitt and wash bucket before washing the fender. You may need to rinse the mitt with clear water to remove embedded grit. There should be no need to spray Simple Green on the fender, wash soap is usually sufficient. Accumulations of grime around attaching screws are dislodged with a paintbrush.

If the front fender sits high enough off the wheel, try to squeeze the mitt in between them. Rotate the front wheel to force the mitt around, thus washing the inside of the fender. In some cases, the fender is mounted much too closely for the mitt to fit. For those, dip a thin towel into the wash bucket, wring it out and fold it into a tight bundle. If that doesn't work either, attempt to clean as much of the underside of the fender as possible with a floppy paintbrush.

Depending on the style of your motorcycle, wash the headlight next, or save it for the section involving the top of the bike or the fairing. It is washed with the mitt, paintbrush and toothbrush as needed. A paintbrush is great for removing bug residue and the dirty film that forms between the light lens, light ring and housing. Washing inside that groove makes the entire headlight look crisp. Stubborn bug or road oil residue on the glass lens is removed with a light touch of the SOS pad or #0000 steel wool and liquid wax. Rinse as often as necessary with clear water to prevent soap from drying on the surface of the headlight housing, fuel tank or fender.

Cables are quickly cleaned with the wash mitt. Put the mitt on your hand and grab the cable with it. Then, just run your hand down the length of the cable. Use a toothbrush on the metal ends.

The way in which you section your motorcycle for cleaning is up to you. After washing the front wheel, you can choose to wash the fairing and headlight area. Or, move on to the rear wheel for extensive cleaning at that area. This Electra Glide was ridden in rainy weather and is covered with a road-water film. Paintbrush cleaning is a must for removing dirt and grime from all the various nooks and crannies.

Fenders seldom need the cleaning strength of cleaner, especially if they have been maintained with a good coat of wax. Instead, use plenty of foam from the wash bucket and a continuous light wipe with a soft cotton wash mitt. Even the most stubborn bug residue will loosen up after a while.

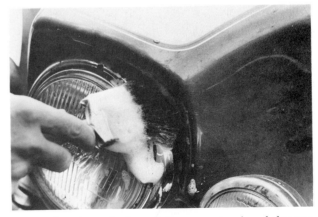

A paintbrush worked great for removing bug leftovers and road-water residue from the headlight trim ring section of this Harley. Note the duct tape wrapped around the metal band on the brush. This protected the fairing from paint chips during vigorous cleaning.

Rear assembly

Rear wheels are cleaned much like the front ones. The tire, rim, spokes, axle hub, brake assembly and cables require the same basic attention. Access is limited due to the swing arm, chain and rear sprocket, and you will have to be persistent in your cleaning efforts. Rotating the rear wheel may be more difficult, there is more weight in the rear when the bike is on the center stand. This may require moving the bike ahead a few feet at a time in order to gain access to the entire wheel circumference.

After the basic wheel assembly has been cleaned, rinse with water and move on to the swing arm. Wash as much as you can with the mitt and follow up with a paintbrush. You will be surprised at how much dirt comes loose with just a slight agitation of the soft bristles. Use a paintbrush along the edges of factory stickers placed on this piece. Clean, crisp edges will make stickers look new.

Be sure to wash under the swing arm, as well as the inner edge next to the wheel. The area directly under the front part of the fender should not be overlooked either. Once again, use a paintbrush or toothbrush around nuts and bolts.

The rear fender is cleaned just like the front. Try to clean the underside of the fender as well. Use a paintbrush to reach those areas just under the sides of the seat. If the seat has been removed, take advantage of long paintbrush bristles to reach tight areas between the fender and frame. A light flow of water is all that is needed for rinsing.

Taillights are not much of a cleaning problem. The wash mitt reaches most of them with ease. Use a toothbrush to scrub away wax that was inadvertently smudged into the tiny letters on the light lens. A toothbrush is also handy for removing build-up inside the heads of Phillips screws attaching the taillight cover to the base. Other tight spots are cleaned with the paintbrush.

For best cleaning results, remove the license plate. This gives you access to the back of the plate and the area of the fender that was covered by it. Use various brushes as necessary.

Shock absorbers can be very difficult to clean. The outer spring makes it almost impossible to clean the inner cylinder. A meticulous detailer

Dan Mycon's Sportster does not have a center stand. To reach all parts of the rear wheel and tire, Art Wentworth had to move the bike a few feet ahead. Be careful, as the ground will be wet and slippery.

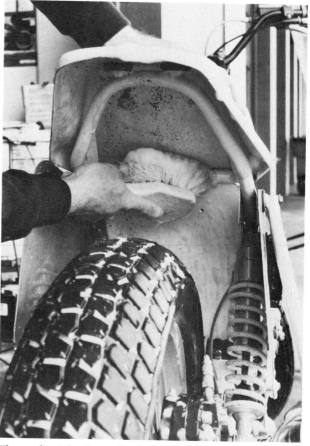

The underside of rear fenders should be cleaned as well as possible. This fender on Squire Tomasie's Flat Tracker poses no access problem. A plastic-bristled brush was used to break loose stubborn racetrack debris.

will spend a lot of time with a small towel, attempting to reach inside the spring for cleaning. A simpler method entails using a long-bristled paintbrush with plenty of suds from the wash bucket. Dab and twist the paintbrush around the entire shock from top to bottom. You will have to maneuver the brush between each of the spring's rings for complete coverage. This is a bit time consuming, but much easier than dismantling both units. Use a toothbrush around bolts as needed.

The chain, chain guard and rear sprocket will surely need cleaning, provided your motorcycle is equipped with them. Wally Shearer washes these parts on his dirt bike after every ride. Instead of Gunk, solvent or soap, he uses WD-40.

Others, like Ralph Maughn, prefer to clean their chains with kerosene. Afterward, they may touch them up with a paintbrush, soap and water. O-ring chains, on the other hand, must be cleaned with care. Harsh petroleum-based cleaners can damage the small rubber O-rings and render the chain useless. Manufacturers recommend they be cleaned with kerosene and then properly lubricated. It may be wise to check with your motorcycle dealer to find out what precautions are in order for the specific type of chain on your bike.

The chain guard and sprocket can also be cleaned with kerosene. Any remaining film is washed off with soap and water. The rear wheel will have to be rotated in order to reach the entire chain and all of the teeth on the sprocket. Use extreme caution while moving the wheel to avoid injury to fingers and hands. If necessary, just move the bike ahead a few feet at a time to rotate the tire, sprocket and chain.

Outer springs on shock absorbers make it difficult to clean the shock body. Before resorting to shock absorber dismantling, try a paintbrush with plenty of soapsuds. You may be pleasantly surprised at the results.

With the saddlebag removed, access is improved to the side area of the rear fender. Once again, a paintbrush is quite handy for crisp cleaning around bolts and brackets.

Gunk and other solvents can be used to remove grease and chain lube accumulations at the rear wheel. This area on bikes with O-ring chains should be cleaned with kerosene, since it will not dry out or otherwise harm the O-rings. Kerosene is recommended by O-ring chain manufacturers.

After the engine has been sprayed with cleaner, use the wash mitt to bring in plenty of soapsuds. Work the mitt around as best you can and then use a paintbrush.

Sides

At the conclusion of chain and sprocket cleaning, you should rinse the wash bucket and tools again. By now, you will have collected grit in the bucket and the water will be dirty. Rinse the mitt and all of the brushes with clear water and mix up a new bucket of soapy water.

Working on one side at a time, liberally spray cleaner over the entire side of the engine. Then, use the wash mitt to put on a thick layer of soapsuds. Agitate a floppy paintbrush in between the fins on the cylinder from top to bottom. Scrub the carburetor and air intake hoses with a toothbrush. Move down to the cases and wash them thoroughly, using brushes and SOS pads as needed.

Bill Buckingham specializes in BMW motorcycles. For years, he has cleaned the fins on horizontal cylinder heads with a non-metallic parts brush. The stiff, non-scratching brush works very well to remove harsh, baked-on debris. It is important to reiterate that this brush is *not* a wire parts brush, but one with stout, plastic bristles.

Lots of soapsuds and long bristles from a paintbrush make a good combination for cleaning deep into engine fins. Concentrate on a small section of the engine at a time to ensure adequate cleaning. Moving too fast will result in missed areas and the need to go over the entire section a second time.

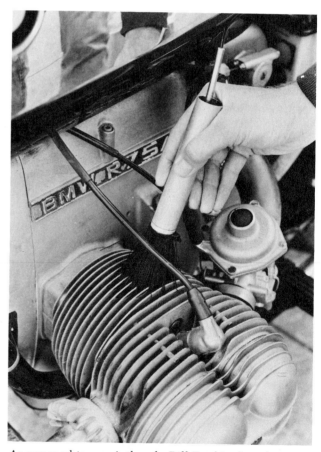

As opposed to a paintbrush, Bill Buckingham has successfully used this plastic-type parts brush on BMW engines for a long time. The stout stature of these bristles makes quick work of removing baked-on debris caught in the fins of protruding BMW cylinders.

Now, if the engine was exceptionally clean to begin with, there may not be a need to use a brush or cleaner. Car wash soap or dish soap alone may do a fine job. Test an area before resorting to stiff brushes and SOS pads. If the mitt and paintbrush do the job, then so be it.

Carburetors on dirt bikes collect dirt along the seam between the upper and lower sections. A toothbrush works well to remove that dirt, most of the time. In special cases, you may have to try an SOS pad to get them really clean. This also holds true for the clamps that hold on air cleaner hoses.

Carburetors on sport bikes tend to stay cleaner. For the most part, cleaning them with a paintbrush is sufficient. As with all carburetors, there is no need to rinse them with copious amounts of water. A very slight and gentle stream of water is all that is needed.

Wires are cleaned with soap and water. They are easiest to clean with the mitt, the same way you cleaned the cables. A toothbrush is used to brighten spark plug caps on ignition wires. Extra-dirty wires are cleaned with solvent and paper towels. Just dab a little solvent on the towel, lay it

Accessible air cleaner housings are washed, but you must take care that water is not directed into the housing itself. Cleaning this part at this time is only necessary for those housings suffering a great deal of dust and dirt build-up. Light dust and dirt accumulations can be cleaned later.

A toothbrush is exceptionally useful for cleaning carburetor bodies. The short bristles reach into corners of the bowl and around Phillips head screws. Spray cleaner and scrub with a toothbrush for maximum cleaning efforts.

across your hand and then pinch the wire between your fingers. Run your hand down the wire a few times until all of the dirt is gone. Follow that with a thorough wash with soap and water to remove remaining traces of solvent, as it could eventually dry out the wire's protective outer coat.

Accessible air cleaner housings are washed with the mitt and paintbrush. Don't be too aggressive with rinse water; water may be forced into the element or even into the carburetor. You may even hit the bike with just the right trajectory and end up with water bouncing back all over you. Always try to remember that gentle is best when detailing. The milder the method, the easier it is on the machine and the detailer.

Raised exhaust pipes are washed just like those designed with lower profiles. Access is limited on some dirt bikes because the pipes are tucked in and out of the way. Clean those pipes the best you can during this phase. Later, during detailed cleaning, you may want to remove this pipe in order to thoroughly clean it and the areas that it was blocking. Sanding and repainting is much easier with it off the bike. Continue cleaning all of that part of the bike including foot levers, frame and engine.

Top

Once again, check the condition of the wash bucket, mitt and brushes. Rinse and freshen as necessary. The fuel tank is washed with plenty of foam on the wash mitt. Be sure to wash the underside, as it tends to collect more dirt than the top. Easily removed tanks are taken off so that their underside can be washed, as well as the frame, wires and top

Exposed air cleaner housings, like this one on Ralph Maughn's Yamaha, must be protected from water during the wash. A piece of plastic was used here to prevent water from entering the air cleaner box during the initial wash of Maughn's bike.

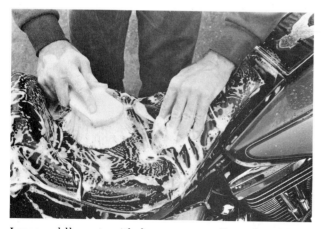

Large saddle seats with deep creases collect a lot of dust, lint and dirt. Heavy cleaning is done with a plastic brush. Use your free hand to stretch the material and open creases for cleaning.

Dirt accumulations are removed from the bottom of seats with a paintbrush. Holes in the bottom plate expose seat padding, so use the least amount of water necessary for cleaning to prevent pads from becoming soaked. Too much moisture collected in the pad may cause mildew and rot.

of the engine underneath them. When rinsing the tank, take care not to force water around the cap area, as water could leak into the tank.

Heavily soiled seats are scrubbed with the plastic-bristled brush. A toothbrush is used along the bead and around buttons. On soft seats with pleats, use your free hand to stretch the material and open the folds. You will be surprised at how much dirt accumulates in these folds.

Seats on hinges should be opened to allow access to the underside and parts below. Use a damp mitt to wipe away dust. A paintbrush with lots of suds is just right for cleaning the tops of batteries, wiring loops and exposed fender and air cleaner parts. If the seat is easy to remove, take it off. This will provide excellent access to that part of the motorcycle for cleaning.

Windshields are made of materials that scratch. It is best to clean them with a soft mitt and mild soap. Stubborn encrusted spots of bug residue are removed with plastic polish after three or four failed attempts with the wash mitt and soap. Be sure to wash the inside of the windshield as well as the edges and supporting brackets.

Fairings come in a variety of sizes and shapes. The Suzuki Katana features a full, wraparound sport fairing much like the Kawasaki Ninja. It has to be removed before any detailed engine cleaning can take place. The Harley-Davidson full fairing allows the engine to be plainly visible. Rory Vance likes to remove the fairing from his Katana at least twice a year. He does this to clean the engine and inside the fairing.

The very front lower part of the sport fairing takes a beating from road hazards and dirt thrown up by the front tire. Cleaning alone may not be successful, you will probably have to polish this piece for maximum effects. A good coat of wax will help to protect it against chips and stains.

Washing fairings is best accomplished with a soapy mitt and floppy paintbrush. The inside of full fairings, like those on Harley-Davidson machines, must also be cleaned. Soap and water work fine. Use caution with the rinse water, though. A

The wraparound fairing on Rory Vance's Katana sport bike does a good job of protecting the engine from dust and dirt. Twice a year is not too often to remove the lower fairing and clean the engine. It can be done more often, depending upon your preference.

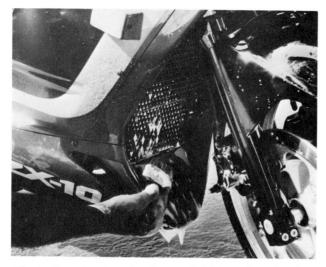

The bottom front parts of sport fairings take a beating from road hazards thrown up by the front tire. Clean this area often to prevent road grime build-up. Frequent waxing helps protect paint.

gentle stream of water is all that is needed to float suds and dirt away.

The instrument cluster and triple clamp are intricate areas to clean. Once again, a paintbrush proves to be the best cleaning tool. There is no need to soak these parts with a lot of water. A paintbrush loaded with foam is sufficient to loosen dirty films, and a gentle rinsing prevents water from causing any damage. Stubborn dirt around the triple clamp is sprayed with S100, Simple Green or other heavy-duty cleaner before scrubbing with the paintbrush. Give the cleaner a few moments to soak in and then

agitate with the paintbrush. Grease build-up at cable connections under the gauges is removed with a toothbrush and cleaner.

Handlebars are cleaned with the wash mitt. Chrome bars may be lightly scrubbed with an SOS pad to remove rust stains or other unique problems. Afterward, remember to put a light coat of wax on the bars to help prevent rust stains from re-appearing.

Handgrips are scrubbed with the toothbrush. Unusually dirty grips may have to be scrubbed with the plastic-bristled brush and a powdered cleanser. If they are too far gone, plan on replacing them with new ones. They are inexpensive and cannot be repaired.

Bare metal hand levers seldom become heavily soiled. However, on those rare occasions, an SOS pad works well to brighten them. Don't use an SOS pad on painted levers, though, as the pad may wear through paint. Instead, try a toothbrush and cleaner.

Hand-operated controls on the handlebars, such as intercom buttons and turn-signal switches, can become layered with a dirty film after extended operation. The oils on your thumb and from gloves tend to cause a greasy build-up to form around these mechanisms. Clean them gently with a toothbrush that has been sprayed with cleaner. Use a slight stream of water for rinsing in order to prevent moisture from entering into the switches.

Mirrors and turn-signal lights should not be overlooked during the initial wash. Bug residue left behind after washing with the mitt is removed with a light application of an SOS pad. Use a paint-

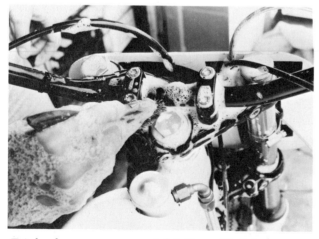

Triple-clamp areas present detailers with tight quarters and a number of items to clean. Access is limited and best achieved by a small paintbrush. A small cloth works well to clean cables, and a toothbrush may be just the thing to clean dirt from Allen head screws and bolts.

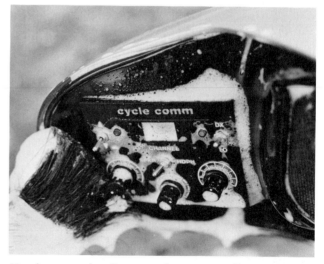

Hand-operated radio controls are generally intricate. It is almost impossible to do a thorough cleaning job without the use of a paintbrush or toothbrush. Gentle scrubbing works fine and will limit the possibility of damage to rather fragile switches. Rinsing is accomplished with a light stream of water.

brush to wash down the mirror and the housing for that extra-crisp look. Try a toothbrush on the screw heads and lettering on the light lens. Rinse with clear water.

Extras

Saddlebags are easiest to clean while off the bike. Because fiberglass and plastic bags scratch, set them on top of a plastic wash bucket while you wash with the mitt. You can also rest them on the lawn or other soft surface. Use a paintbrush or toothbrush along edges and seams.

Leather saddlebags should be cleaned and treated with the products recommended by the manufacturer or distributor. You can use all-purpose leather products like Lexol without much worry of causing stains or blemishes. Heavily soiled bags that won't clean with gentle methods may require the use of saddle soap.

Leather bags that have gotten wet should be removed, stuffed with newspaper and allowed to sit in a warm, dry place. After they have dried, brush off grit and dirt with a soft brush. Then, treat them with a coat of Lexol, Hide Food or other leather

Washing the instrument panel on this Electra Glide was accomplished with a paintbrush and plenty of soap-suds. Instead of blasting water at the panel to remove suds, a gentle stream of water was provided by turning down the faucet. The light water stream prevented excess water from entering radio speakers, and prevented moisture from entering the instrument panel face.

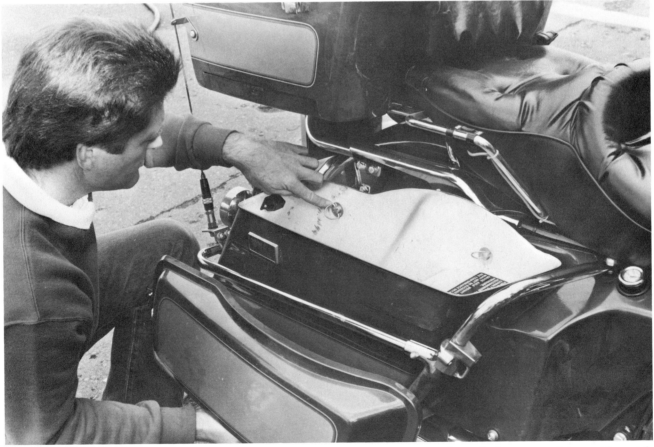

Saddlebags are easiest to clean while they are off of the motorcycle. Harley-Davidson bags on this Electra Glide come loose with just a twist of the pins. Place saddlebags on a cloth or towel, not the bare ground, to avoid scratch problems.

Leather saddlebags should be cleaned and dressed with products recommended by the manufacturer. In this case, Peter Danikas recommends Mother's Preserves for conditioning this leather sissy bar bag.

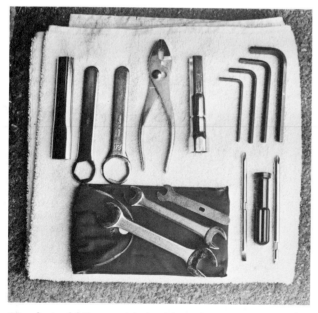

Handy tool kits provided with many new motorcycles are heaven-sent when a plug fouls or an item comes loose while on a road trip or outing. Check your tool kit once a month to be sure all the tools are still there and in working condition.

care product as recommended by the manufacturer. If you are still concerned about the correct type of conditioner to use, check with a local leather shop for their specific recommendations. Leather and accessories will be covered in more detail in Chapter 11.

Tool kits are provided with just about every new motorcycle. These handy accessories provide almost every tool a rider needs to make emergency repairs to his or her motorcycle. It is safe to say that when you need them, you really need them. Take a few minutes to remove the kit and place all of the tools out in the open. Wipe the wrenches and screwdriver set with the mitt and then with a clean towel lightly dabbed in WD-40. Then do the same to the pliers, making sure they open and close with ease. Clean the pliable vinyl case, and apply a light coat of Armor All or other polypenetrant.

Harley-Davidson motorcycles feature some unique and intricate emblems, insignias and gas caps. This special metal work presents rather unique cleaning problems. Reaching deep into the grooves and valleys of these specialty items is not easy. About the only tools that have proved successful are toothbrushes and cotton swabs.

Dan Mycon takes special pleasure in his new Sportster and has spent a few extra dollars on goodies, one of which is a special Harley-Davidson fuel cap. The ornate badge on top of the cap accumulated lots of dirt, making it look dull and old. Car wash soap and a little Simple Green on an old toothbrush cleaned out the valleys and made the badge look new again. To dry the cap, Mycon used a cotton swab and a blow dryer. This prevented water drops from dribbling on the tank, causing water spots and streaks.

Fuel tank caps come in various sizes, shapes and designs. Dan Mycon opted for an ornate Harley-Davidson cap on his Sportster. The only way to clean between the ridges on this cap is with a toothbrush.

Hard-to-reach areas

When you squat down and look closely at a motorcycle, you'll notice that there are literally hundreds of little spaces where dirt accumulates, and in which your hand or fingers will not fit. They have to be cleaned, but how?

Novice motorcycle enthusiasts have spent countless hours using the fold of a cloth to reach these places in an attempt to clean them to perfection. This is certainly a successful method, but painstakingly difficult. A much quicker and simpler method employs a floppy paintbrush and soft toothbrush. Occasionally, a cotton swab fits the bill.

Detailers must constantly be on the lookout for new and improved methods for cleaning automotive machinery. Since nobody has yet invented the perfect spray-on, rinse-off miracle cleaner, we must all rely on ingenuity and elbow grease.

Use your imagination and ingenuity to clean the unique spaces on your bike. Insert the handle of the toothbrush into a towel to rigidly clean between the fins on the cylinder of your Yamaha. Use a baby bottle brush to clean inside the tight spaces

Reaching around crowded exhaust pipes is not always easy. To ensure total coverage, Wentworth uses the wash mitt like a shoe shine buffing cloth, moving along the pipe to clean the backside.

To get a good handle on how the wash job is coming along, you have to squat down and carefully look at all parts of the motorcycle. Art Wentworth is inspecting the front of this Electra Glide for areas missed after the first rinse. Further cleaning is done with the wash mitt and paintbrush.

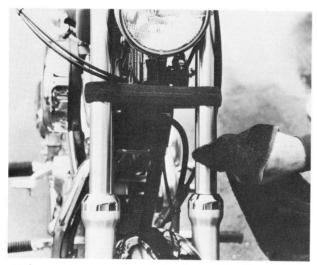

At the onset, use two towels for drying. The first one will absorb most of the water, and the second will pick up lingering moisture. This towel is being used to completely dry the fork tubes on Mycon's Sportster.

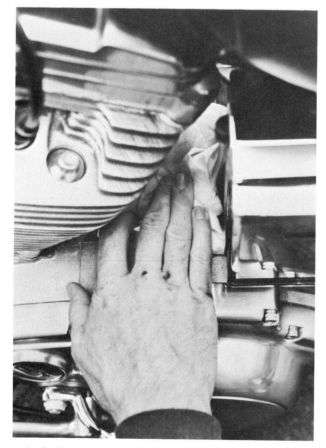

Soft, fluffy cotton towels may be too thick to reach into corners for complete drying. For those, try paper towels. The thin texture and excellent absorbing power of paper towels are great for getting water out of corners and from under tight-fitting brackets.

around the triple clamp. You can even use your bare fingers to clean the chrome rim around spoked wheel nipples. Mycon says to do whatever you have to do, just get it clean!

Reaching inside the spokes of the rear wheel on a touring motorcycle is not easy. You may have to use a one-inch-wide paintbrush to clean an inch at a time. The other option is removing the wheel, which may not be a bad idea on a yearly basis.

Some dismantling may be required. You be the judge. If a part is difficult to reach, but desperately needs cleaning, consider removing it.

Drying

Motorcycles should *never* be put away wet. Condensation forms in the exhaust pipes and can travel into the engine, and water settles on various parts and may cause corrosion. It is best you do a good job of drying your bike after each thorough wash.

Initially, use two towels for drying: one to pick up large puddles and one to wipe away residual moisture. Start at the top and work down. Be sure to reach under the fuel tank and inside fairing ports. Wipe off the seat and the space underneath. Dry the swing arm and shocks, wheel rim and fender.

When most of the water has been removed, start the engine and let it idle. Once it reaches operating temperature, or when the choke is no longer needed, take it for a quick spin up the street. Avoid mud puddles and oil slicks, all you are trying to do is blow off excess water.

This helps to dry the bike in preparation for detailed cleaning, and gets unwanted water out of exhaust pipes, engine fins, wheels, spoke nipples, brake parts and so forth.

When you return, use a towel to pick up any lingering water droplets or streaks. This prevents the formation of water spots. If stubborn water accumulations persist, use a corner of the towel to absorb and remove them. This is most common on top of the engine case behind the cylinder head and under the seat. Stubborn water deposits in tight grooves and seams are wicked up with a paper towel. As a last resort, employ Mycon's trick and use a blow dryer to get rid of moisture in inaccessible spaces.

The bottom line is getting the bike as dry as possible before applying wax or attempting to perform detailed cleaning on particular areas. In all cases, it is imperative that the motorcycle be completely dry before storing for any extended period. This greatly reduces the risk of corrosion and rust problems.

Chapter 4

Engine and exhaust

The engine should be quite clean after an initial wash. For most enthusiasts, this is acceptable as a monthly spiff. Once or twice a year, though, these meticulous motorcyclists will detail their engines to perfection.

An annual or semi-annual engine detail not only makes the entire bike look better, but also helps the machine maintain a higher-than-average resale value, and gives you the chance to thoroughly inspect every square inch of the cases, cylinder head, carburetor, linkages, wires, hoses, radiator and exhaust pipes. Motorcycles vibrate, albeit some more than others, which periodically causes nuts, bolts and screws to loosen. This is an excellent time to torque all such fasteners to manufacturers' specifications.

Dismantling

Parts around the engine and exhaust may have to be removed before detailed cleaning begins. The degree to which you need to dismantle is up to you. Full-fairing sport bikes naturally need the fairing taken off, just to see the engine.

Fuel tanks on dirt bikes come off quickly and easily, and should be removed for detailed cleaning. Others, like those on large touring bikes, may be too complicated and cumbersome to remove and you may have to work around them.

Guards protecting the chain and sprocket at the engine can be taken off in order to clean the sprocket and surrounding area. This will be a dirty task and you might consider doing this during the initial wash. At that time, major cleaning can be accomplished. Afterward, detailed cleaning can take place.

Foot levers and pegs generally do not present any special cleaning problems. If they are extra

Ralph Maughn used this makeshift center stand to support his Yamaha during detailed cleaning and part replacement. Definitive engine care included chain removal, sprocket cleaning and some paint work.

The lower fairing on this sport bike had to be taken off in order to gain access to the engine for cleaning. Because the engine is in decent shape, further dismantling is not called for. Other motorcycle styles may require additional dismantling for the once or twice a year super detail. The choice is left up to you and your degree of enthusiasm.

Engine detailing cannot be accomplished with full sport fairings in place. Even with the lower fairing removed from Rory Vance's Katana, access to the top of the engine was still somewhat limited. You have to make do with what you have. In this case, Simple Green was applied through a vent in the upper fairing.

dirty, remove them to be cleaned in a bucket of soapy water with a plastic brush. An SOS pad will help to remove stubborn build-up. While they are off the bike, clean the areas where they were attached and the connection rods they were attached to.

Skid plates collect a lot of grease, dirt and grime. It is not a bad idea to remove and clean them once or twice a year. Use a paper towel to pick up large accumulations of debris and then just throw it away. Further cleaning is done with cleaner, wash mitt, paintbrush, toothbrush and plastic brush as needed. If the nuts and bolts attaching the skid plate to the frame are heavily covered with grease and grime, soak them in a can of solvent and then scrub with a toothbrush. Treat them to a light coat of WD-40 after drying, to keep rust or corrosion from occurring.

Detailed cleaning
Engine
Engine cleaning and service work is easy on most bikes because the motor is out in the open. Newer sport and touring models present a slight problem, however, in that fairings cover much of the engine. It is impossible to detail an engine with the fairing in place, you will have to remove it. Take your time and use the correct tools. Lay a soft blanket on the ground under the fairing to protect it from scratches during removal.

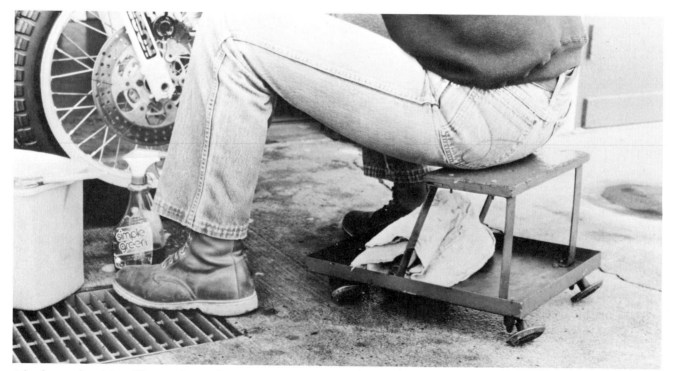

A brake mechanic's rolling stool is perfect to sit on while detailing a motorcycle engine. Not only is it the right height, but it also has a shelf to store cleaning and detailing supplies.

This work can be done on the driveway or in a well-lit garage. There should be no need for running water since detailed cleaning will be done with a damp cloth and paper towels, toothbrush, spray bottle of cleaner, cotton swabs and possibly some very fine steel wool.

Park your bike on the center stand and use a bucket or stool to sit on. If your dirt bike is not equipped with a center stand, devise a makeshift support that it can rest on. Bigger bikes, such as Electra Glides, will have to remain on the side stand. Use caution so that vigorous cleaning doesn't knock over the machine. A stool is a real back saver while performing this kind of work. Squire Tomasie uses a brake mechanic's stool on wheels and says it is ideal. It rolls easily and has a shelf under the seat to hold cleaning and polishing supplies.

Before you begin cleaning, you might want to check out the air cleaner. Elements that have not been replaced or serviced in a long time will probably be covered with dust and dirt. When they are removed, they will naturally cause some dirt and dust to fall on the engine. It makes sense to remove them before the engine is detailed.

Certain K&N reusable air filters are guaranteed for a million miles, as long as they are maintained according to the manufacturer's recommendations. Nate Shelton of K&N Engineering Incorporated, says that many people clean this filter far too often, and that under normal highway conditions this filter should not need cleaning for 35,000–50,000 miles. He goes on to say that the filter actually cleans the air better when it is a bit dirty. Cleaning is not necessary until the wire mesh covering the filtering media is no longer visible.

Start cleaning at the top of the engine. Use a damp towel to wipe off excess water or dirt. A close inspection may reveal tiny bits of dirt caught in the grooves around recessed bolt holes and the seams between the head and barrel. Lightly dampen the bristles of a toothbrush with cleaner, and scrub those areas. For extra-stubborn greasy spots, the toothbrush can be dampened with Gunk or solvent. A damp towel is all you will need to wipe away residue.

Reaching inside the fins on a motorcycle engine is difficult. A paintbrush works well, and so does the handle of a toothbrush inserted inside a cleaning cloth.

On finned heads, you may have to use cotton swabs to reach deep into valleys to remove dirt and grime. A small damp towel placed over the end of a plastic toothbrush handle also works well to wipe off dirt stains and water spots from fin faces. The job of cleaning is not hard, it is the effort exerted to reach out-of-the-way nooks and crannies that is difficult.

When the cylinder fins have been cleaned, look at the carburetor and the attachments on it. The clamp holding the air cleaner hose may be dull and caked with dirt next to the screw mechanism. Light cleaning is done with a toothbrush. More intense cleaning and polishing will require removing the clamp. An SOS pad works great for shining dull clamps. Before you put it back on, lightly coat the screw with WD-40 and be sure to wipe off excess.

Old-looking and stained carburetors are lightly scrubbed with a damp SOS pad for rejuvenation. The pad is quite pliable, and you can use a thin edge to clean the seam between the body of the carburetor and the bowl on the bottom. A toothbrush works very well to clean the Phillips head screws at the bottom of the bowl. Lay a paper towel

Clamps on carburetors collect dust and dirt. A toothbrush works well to break loose most accumulations. In some cases, you may have to remove the clamps for definitive cleaning off the bike. After washing, apply a light coat of WD-40 or other lubricant to screws.

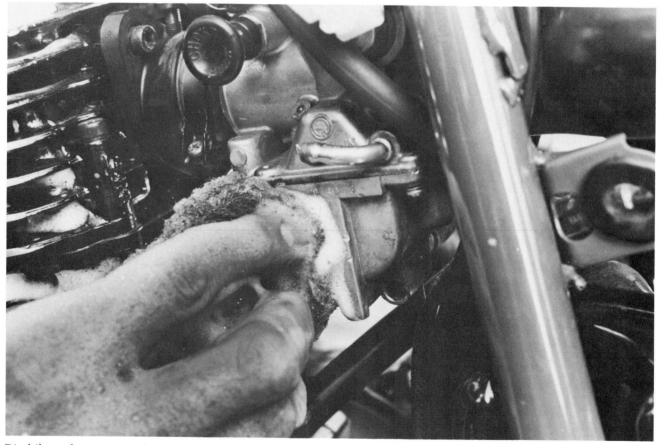

Dirt bike carburetors get plenty dirty, sometimes defying the most vigorous toothbrush scrubbing. Here, an SOS pad is used to thoroughly clean a carburetor body. Note that the fuel inlet tube is open and uncovered. A piece of duct tape should be placed over it to prevent water from entering the carburetor.

over the engine case below the carburetor to catch dripping soapsuds and residue.

The top of the carburetor is intricate and not so easy to clean. Try a paintbrush sprayed with cleaner, use a toothbrush as necessary. You can even use the folds of a folded paper towel to reach into slots next to the throttle cable. On multicylinder bikes, you will have to do the best you can to reach all of the carburetors. Consider removing the fuel tank for the once or twice a year detail. This will give you better access not only to clean, but also to inspect the carburetors.

Air cleaner hoses also need cleaning. A small cloth moistened with cleaner should remove almost anything missed during the initial wash. Tough stains are scrubbed with a toothbrush, extra-tough spots may have to be lightly scoured with an SOS pad. Be sure to check the other end of the carburetor too, the part that attaches to the engine. Use a toothbrush as necessary.

Place a small cloth over your hand and spray some cleaner on it. Then, pinch fuel lines and cables between your fingers for thorough cleaning. The metal end of cables and the base of fuel lines are best cleaned with a toothbrush.

Engine cases generally are broad and easy to clean. Meticulous work may require using a toothbrush to clean the edges of recessed lettering on the side cases next to the shift and rear brake levers. Bolt recesses collect a lot of dirt and road grime. Spray them with cleaner and scrub with a paintbrush. Use a toothbrush for stubborn build-up.

Allen head screws and bolts also collect dirt. Residue left behind after scrubbing with a toothbrush is cleaned by twisting a cotton swab inside the head. Greasy residue may require you to dip the cotton swab in solvent before application. A clean cotton swab is inserted afterward to absorb remaining solvent residue.

Spend an adequate amount of time cleaning one side of the engine. As you work, you will notice yourself stretching around the front and back sides. But don't get too carried away; you will be able to reach those areas from the other side. Clean as much as you can comfortably reach.

Each side of the engine will present unique features. Ralph Maughn's Yamaha TT 600 K has a compression release on the right side which will require extra cleaning attention. The left side presents the chain and sprocket as an extra cleaning chore. Give the added items their required amount of cleaning time before racing to the other side.

Exhaust pipes

Once a year, Bill Buckingham pulls the stainless steel exhaust pipe off of his BMW and has it professionally polished. A bit eccentric, perhaps, but he appreciates his motorcycle and takes exceptionally good care of it. He is rewarded with a good-

Intricate detailing may call for use of a cotton swab. These are handy items that can be used in a number of places. This swab is absorbing dirt and water residue from the base of recessed letters on an engine side cover in preparation for painting.

looking machine that operates as expected and retains a very high dollar value.

Exhaust pipes always need cleaning, whether they are chrome, black chrome, painted flat black or stainless. Most of the time, washing with a cleaner, like Simple Green, and a wash mitt is suf-

The compression release on the right side of Ralph Maughn's Yamaha needs cleaning. Scrubbing with a paintbrush and toothbrush will remove most of the dirt and caked-on residue. This is an extra item presented on the right side of the engine; the left side will sport its own unique items for cleaning.

ficient. On those with clamps and guards, use a paintbrush to remove build-up and grime from Phillips heads, seams and ridges. In some cases, it is best to remove the heat shield. This gives you easy access to that part of the pipe covered by it, and will allow you to clean the shield on both sides. Use a toothbrush as necessary.

Stubborn spots of baked-on dirt and road debris are removed with a light touch of an SOS pad. If you are concerned that this soap pad may scratch the exhaust pipe on your bike, make the initial application on an inconspicuous spot first. If the results are satisfactory, you can continue. If not, you will have to try polishing with Simichrome or other mild chrome polish.

Rory Vance has lightly used an SOS pad to clean the black chrome pipes on his Katana with good success. These pads have also been successfully used on the stainless pipe on Buckingham's K100, chrome pipes on Dan Mycon's Sportster and

the flat black pipe on Ralph Maughn's TT dirt bike. The key is in the light touch. If you were to scour the pipe as you would an old frying pan, you would certainly scratch it. Gently scrub the baked-on blemish until it is gone, rinse frequently and check the results. It is much better to spend a few minutes lightly cleaning than to take fifteen seconds scouring and scratching.

Once a year, it is not a bad idea to remove the exhaust pipes from your bike. This gives you the chance to clean areas behind the pipes and to thoroughly clean, polish and/or paint the entire exhaust system. Exhaust pipes are not hard to remove as long as you use the proper tools and take your time.

Exhaust tips suffer black carbon build-up and should be cleaned periodically. It is not necessary to reach deep inside the pipe to clean, just the outer end where build-up is most visible. This is especially noticeable on the flat ends of BMW pipes and the angled tips of Harley-Davidson models. A damp paper towel works best as a first resource. It will collect a lot of dirty residue initially, and is then thrown away. After that, put plenty of soapsuds on a paintbrush and scrub the tip. Use the least amount of water as possible for rinsing.

A light touch with an SOS pad quickly cleaned baked-on dirt residue from the black chrome exhaust pipes of Vance's Katana. Aggressive scouring may scratch black chrome, so opt for a number of light applications as opposed to one or two heavy doses. If you are in doubt as to the use of a steel wool soap pad on your pipes, try one on an inconspicuous place first to see how well it works.

BMW stainless steel exhaust tips also suffer from carbon build-up. Cleaning this tip will improve the overall appearance of the exhaust pipe and rear assembly.

Stubborn build-up is removed with an SOS pad. Rinse again with little water and dry with paper towels. Avoid using too much water as it will pool inside the pipe and cause corrosion. After cleaning is complete, start up the bike to dry the pipes. Be extra alert as to the direction in which the pipes are pointing when you start the bike. Filthy water residue may be forced out of them and splattered against something—or someone—you didn't intend to spray.

Radiator

Don Perry's Honda Gold Wing Interstate is water cooled. Rory Vance's Suzuki Katana has an oil cooler. Both bikes are different, but both have radiators that need periodic cleaning to achieve maximum cooling results.

Motorcycles are designed with radiators at the front to take full advantage of the passing airflow. The system works satisfactorily, but radiators take a beating from road hazards and debris thrown up by the front tire. Bill Buckingham has painstakingly used a tiny screwdriver to remove embedded pebbles from the fins of radiators. He has also taken the time to straighten those fins, using a flat screwdriver and needle-nose pliers.

Most of the time, radiators are cleaned with a paintbrush, soap and water. Once in a while, you may have to use a toothbrush to dislodge a stubborn wad of bug leftovers. It is a good idea to wash

A few minutes cleaning this exhaust tip made a big difference in its overall appearance. It is this kind of attention to detail that makes one bike stand out in comparison to another.

A light touch with a wet SOS pad quickly cleaned the carbon build-up on this BMW exhaust tip without scratching the stainless steel. Very little water was used to rinse off the soapsuds, thus preventing unnecessary moisture from entering the pipe. The bulk of soapsuds was wiped off with a rag.

The oil cooler on Squire Tomasie's Harley is constantly bombarded by racetrack debris. Definitive cleaning is done with a toothbrush, and additional detailing includes straightening the fins and paint touch-up.

this part every time you clean your motorcycle. This practice will not only help the radiator to consistently look good, but will also help to maximize cooling power by allowing smooth and unobstructed airflow.

Wires and hoses

Most of a motorcycle's wiring is hidden under the fuel tank, behind the oil reservoir and in back of the headlight assembly. Only a few wires are exposed, mainly the spark plug ignition wires.

Wires are cleaned individually with a small towel and cleaner. Grease smudges may require the use of solvent, followed by cleaner to remove any solvent residue. A toothbrush is used to remove build-up along the creases and edges of outer jackets covering a number of separate wires.

Some enthusiasts never apply dressing to wires. They choose to leave them clean and bundled in a tidy fashion. Other meticulous motorcyclists like the shiny and rejuvenated appearance brought on by a light coat of Armor All or other dressing. The choice is yours.

Apply dressing in the same manner as you cleaned the wires. Drape the dressing towel over your hand and then pinch the wires between your thumb and forefinger. Run your hand over the length of the wire and be sure to maintain even coverage around its entire circumference. Pull ignition wires off of the spark plugs to ensure even coverage around the cap and next to the ridges on it. The throttle and other cables going to the engine are cleaned and dressed the same way as wires.

Dried, weathered and stained hoses are also treated with a light coat of dressing. If cleaning alone does not bring their appearance up to your standard, try an application of dressing to see if it makes an improvement.

Small hoses, such as fuel lines, are dressed just like wires. Air cleaner hoses and the like will have to be dressed using a different maneuver. Place your forefinger in the dressing towel and spray a bit of dressing on it. Then, carefully apply it to the hose. Avoid smudging metal surfaces surrounding the hose.

Polishing

Motorcycles come with painted and polished engines and exhausts. Some models are designed with a combination. Polishing bare fin faces is just about impossible, as well as impractical. The edges, though, sometimes need attention.

Wentworth's Suzuki features a black engine. Everything is black except outer fin edges. This makes the edges very noticeable and allows them

On Rory Vance's Katana, the oil cooler is protected by the fairing. Definitive cleaning required only dirt and dust removal with a toothbrush.

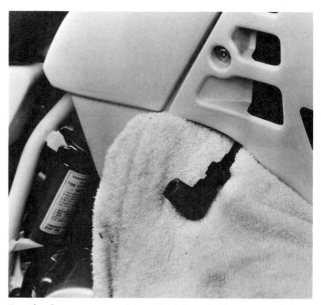

Spark plug caps are cleaned with a cloth. Dirt and dust in the corners are removed with a toothbrush. A little dab of solvent on the cloth will remove grease smears and build-up. You should follow solvent use with a cleaner to remove solvent residue.

The exposed and shiny edges on the fins of Art Wentworth's Suzuki periodically need brightening. In the past, he has used emory cloth with good results. However, a milder and just as effective method employs #600 wet-and-dry sandpaper in lieu of coarse emory cloth.

Bill Buckingham used Ouator Metal Polish & Cleaner to make the bare metal parts on this 1965 BMW R69S look new. Other chrome and mag polishes may have worked just as well. As with any detailing or cleaning product, you have to decide which is best for your needs.

Abrasive chrome polish does not have to be used every time you want to shine chrome. Those chrome pieces that are in excellent shape, such as the air cleaner cover on Dan Mycon's Sportster, can be lightly polished with a mild paint sealer/glaze, and then treated to a light coat of wax for long-lasting protection.

to be a focal point. After extended riding, the edges become dull and dirty. He likes to brighten them periodically to keep them looking crisp.

To do this, Wentworth firmly sands each edge with one or two strokes of #600 wet-and-dry sandpaper. In the past, he has used emory cloth to brighten exceptionally dull fin edges. Emory cloth is very coarse, however, and shouldn't be used except in extreme cases. The #600 wet-and-dry sandpaper does an excellent job without removing too much of the surface. It is much better to apply fine-grit sandpaper three or four times as opposed to harsh emory cloth once or twice.

A number of products are available that will shine dull aluminum engine pieces. The most popular is Happich Simichrome. Eagle 1 Mag & Chrome Polish works well, as do other chrome polishes. Bill Buckingham carries a product called Ouator (pronounced *water*) at his BMW shop. It produced remarkable results on the engine and hand levers of an older BMW undergoing restoration.

The product used is not as important as the care given to its application. Dabbing too much polish on a cloth that is too cumbersome will result in polish residue spread all over the engine. Use a small cloth, about the size of an ordinary bathroom washcloth. Place your index finger inside the cloth and gather just a bit of polish on your fingertip. With controlled application, polish a small section at a time. For instance, polish an inspection cover before moving on to the front of the case. Use seams and recess edges as guides.

Polish in a back-and-forth direction as opposed to a circular motion. This will establish a pattern and a minute grain in the surface, making it free of swirls. In the direct sunlight, polished parts will look uniform and new, not scratched and covered with spider webbing. Use caution around bolt holes. It is easy to fill these recesses with polish, making cleanup more time consuming.

Highly polished engine pieces may not need the coarse treatment of chrome polish. You may have better luck using a mild auto paint glaze or sealer to bring it up to par. Always start with the mildest method first. For bright chrome parts, like Harley air cleaner covers, try something like Meguiar's #7 before using chrome polish. This holds true for engine cases and polished carburetors too.

Use chrome polish to brighten dull chrome and stainless exhaust pipes. Apply polish in a straight back-and-forth direction to avoid swirls. A number of light applications are much better than a single heavy concentration. Wipe off the residue

Mother's Mag & Aluminum Polish did an outstanding job of shining this neglected BMW stainless steel exhaust pipe. Polish was applied only about six inches in *front of and behind the shift lever. Further up the pipe you can see the difference.*

with a clean, soft cloth, again wiping in a straight back-and-forth direction.

Black chrome pipes are beautiful when maintained. Using a coarse chrome polish on them may cause scratching. If a stain persists after washing, try a mild glaze polish before resorting to chrome polish. Art Wentworth has had good results using Meguiar's Car Cleaner Wax to brighten slightly dulled black chrome pipes.

Buffing polish or wax off of pipes can be a tiring chore. To speed the process of removing dry residue from the back side of pipes, slip a soft buffing cloth behind the pipe and grab the end when it clears. Hold an end in each hand and buff the pipe as you would a shoe, or, as you would dry your back with a towel after getting out of the shower.

Anything you polish should also be treated to a coat of wax. Although high temperatures tend to evaporate wax, it never hurts to apply a thin coat to air cleaner housings, engines and exhaust pipes. Polishing removes a slight layer of dulled surface, leaving the new surface bare. Engine cases and ex-

Turtle Wax Polishing Compound was used to shine this neglected black shield on a BMW exhaust pipe. Follow up with a mild polish to remove hairline scratches. A light coat of carnauba may offer some lasting protection.

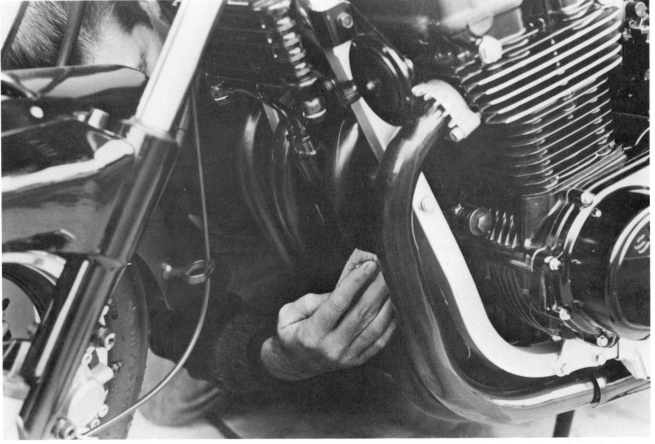

Art Wentworth found it is easiest to apply light polish to exhaust pipes with a small sponge. It is most comfortable for him to polish the far side of pipes as shown in this picture, and then go to the other side of the bike to get the opposite side of the pipes.

The short, stout bristles of the cut-off paintbrush made quick work of removing wax build-up on the engine side case. Follow up with a quick wipe from a soft cloth to remove resultant powder residue.

haust pipes get warm and wax is dissipated, but even a slight residual layer of protective wax can help to protect against water and road hazards.

Polish and wax will undoubtedly build up in seams, recesses and ridges. Use the folded point of a buffing cloth to remove this build-up, or the cut-off paintbrush. The short bristles of this paintbrush have the strength to loosen polish and wax build-up, and are soft enough to use on polished pieces. Just tap the bristles against the build-up and then twist the brush to whisk away residue. Follow with the buffing cloth to remove fine dust left behind.

Painting

Most motorcycle engines are not painted. The few that are, though, may need an occasional touch-up. Luckily, most of the painted engines are black. You can purchase original touch-up paint from the motorcycle shop, or use a heat-resistant paint found at an auto parts store.

Art Wentworth's Suzuki sports a black engine with exposed fin edges. The inspection cover on the right side was scratched during a mishap. Rather than purchase a new cover, he lightly

Masking with wide strips of masking tape and plenty of newspaper prepared the left side of Ralph Maughn's Yamaha engine for selected painting. Due to high temperatures the engine is subjected to, Maughn chose to use heat-resistant paint.

sanded the blemish and masked the cover. He then sprayed the cover to perfection using a semi-gloss heat-resistant paint.

Ralph Maughn took a spill on his dirt bike, resulting in a crack along the inspection cover next to the rear brake lever. Like Wentworth's Suzuki, his Yamaha also sported a black engine. He repaired the crack with liquid steel and then repainted with a flat heat-resistant paint that matched the rest of the engine. The results were excellent. One hardly notices the repair except upon close inspection.

Road grit and sand thrown up by the front tire can easily chip radiator paint. Touch-up is safely done with the small brush that comes with bottles of touch-up paint. You may also opt for masking the area and spray painting the radiator. Since these parts do not get unusually hot, gloss or semi-gloss lacquer paint should work well.

Minor nicks and chips are easiest to repair with the brush-and-bottle method, since masking will not be required and the chips are small. If, however, the radiator has been neglected and is covered with chips and paint blemishes, carefully mask all of the surrounding area and spray the entire radiator. Be sure to mask behind the radiator, as spray paint will pass through the fins and land on the front of the engine. Follow the directions on the label of spray paint you use. Two or more light coats are much better than one heavy coat. Be certain the first coat is dry before applying the second.

Painted pipes are repainted with heat-resistant paint. Although it is best to paint pipes while off of the bike, you can implement some judicious masking and use a paint block with a good degree of success. Ordinary flat black heat-resistant paint is most common on dirt bikes. If your motorcycle has a different color, or, you want a gloss instead of flat, check with the motorcycle shop, auto parts store or local auto body paint and supply store for the right paint.

Engine accessory parts such as battery brackets, air cleaners and levers can also be repainted. Matching touch-up paint can be purchased in the bottle or spray can at motorcycle shops. Various paints are also available at auto parts stores, such as heat-resistant, gloss lacquer and enamel. Color matching may be a problem, as most of these paints are not color-coded to motorcycles.

Each motorcycle has unique features not found on other models. This is a distributor cap on Squire Tomasie's Harley-Davidson Flat Tracker. Not many bikes feature this setup. Caution must be exercised so that water is not forced into the cap. Note the special ties around each ignition wire plug.

Always be sure that parts are properly prepared before painting. This entails a thorough cleaning, sometimes with paint thinner or Prepsol. Solvent-type cleaners will remove any oily film that may be stuck on the part. Such films cause paint to run and may result in fisheye blemishes. Armor All and other dressings will also cause fisheyes and runs. That is why Dan Mycon never applies dressing to any motorcycle part that he thinks may need repainting in the near future.

Keeping it clean

Engine detailing is an intricate task. You can easily spend a day cleaning, polishing and dressing every part of the engine to perfection. So it pays to take steps to keep it clean.

Art Wentworth likes to spray his black Suzuki engine with Armor All, work it in with a paintbrush and then wash it. He says that the remaining dressing makes the engine look brand new. Ralph Maughn sprays the front of his engines with PAM, the baking product used to prevent foods from sticking to frying pans. He says PAM keeps road oil and debris from baking onto the hot engine and makes cleaning an easy chore. Wally Shearer bathes the engines on his dirt bikes with WD-40 af-

Meticulous attention to detail finds many motorcycle enthusiasts doing some pretty unusual things. Dan Mycon really likes his new Sportster and refuses to park it after a wash until it is completely dry. He has gone so far as to use his wife's blow dryer and cotton swabs to remove the last lingering bits of moisture from the engine fins before parking.

ter every ride. The coating prevents dirt from sticking to the engine and is easily rinsed away with a garden hose.

Final remarks

While detailing the motor, you may notice spots away from the engine that need attention. It is perfectly okay to reach over and clean them, as long as you don't get sidetracked. Too many motorcycle detailers will try to concentrate their efforts on one particular area, notice a spot on the tank, then the fairing, mirror and so on. There is nothing wrong with moving around a little bit. A problem arises, though, when you bounce around so much that one area doesn't get the full attention it needs. You soon lose track of what you were doing and find yourself dashing around the motorcycle, doing a little cleaning here and a little there, while nothing gets cleaned completely. This is a waste of time and energy.

Various motorcycles present different cleaning tasks and concerns for their engines. The carburetors on Harley-Davidsons are enclosed under a cover. To reach them, the cover must be removed. Older BMWs feature engine heads that stick out horizontally. They are more apt to pick up road grime and dirt in the fins and carburetors than are other models. Sport bikes with wraparound fairings don't suffer heavy engine soiling except in the front and on the exhaust pipes. Dirt bikes just get dirty all over. You will have to determine how far you want to go with dismantling for detail.

Ralph Maughn has been riding motorcycles for over twenty-five years. He feels that his dirt bikes must be completely disassembled once a year; he takes everything off except the engine. New parts replace worn ones as he sees fit, and everything is cleaned, painted, polished, waxed and serviced. Maughn believes this dedication to detail is the reason his bikes perform well and seldom break down.

Art Wentworth, on the other hand, has never disassembled a motorcycle. Instead, he has always washed his road bikes after every ride. His normal wash includes work with paintbrushes and a toothbrush. It also includes selective waxing, lubrication and bolt checks. Wentworth prefers to stay on top of his bikes all the time, thus relieving him of the need for a complete yearly detail.

When asked how they arrived at their particular methods of engine cleaning and motorcycle detailing, most motorcycle enthusiasts said they got their information from reading about motorcycling and from talking with other enthusiasts. Everyone has their favorite ways of doing things. And the end result is far more important than the means by which the result was achieved. If you have a favorite method for cleaning the engine and exhaust system on your motorcycle, stay with it. Experiment with new ideas as you see fit.

Chapter 5

Wheels, tires and rear assembly

One would think that wheels, tires and brake assemblies should be sparkling clean and detailed after the attention given them during an initial wash. That's true for a weekly or monthly spiff. An annual or semi-annual complete detail, though, will require further cleaning, with some polishing and waxing for wheels, shocks and swing arms, and dressing for tires.

Motorcycle wheels and tires are not always easily accessible. Fairings, fenders and saddlebags make it difficult to reach all parts of the wheel and tire in one position. You will have to remove the obstruction or rotate the wheel in order to clean and polish completely.

Wheels

On the center stand, both wheels can usually be turned by hand. Those bikes featuring side stands only, will have to be rolled back and forth to reposition wheels. Or, for the best possible access, the wheel can be removed and cleaned on a bench.

Uniform cleaning and polishing is important. Just a small spot left unattended on a wheel can be quite an eyesore when the bike is parked with that spot visible.

Most enthusiasts like to start by cleaning and polishing the front wheel first. There is no compelling reason for this, except that it is generally easier to reach and easiest to clean. Start with the dirtiest part first. This way, any residue will be picked up as you move around the wheel.

Chrome-spoked wheels

Chrome-spoked wheels present a lot of individual parts and a lot of surface area to clean. Put soft cotton socks over your hands and use them as cleaning tools, as opposed to a cumbersome towel. No matter what kind of cloth you use, make sure it is a handy size. The dimensions of an ordinary bathroom washcloth are good.

If accumulations of build-up are located along the axle housing, spray cleaner on a small paintbrush and agitate that area until dirt is dislodged. Use a clean paper towel or rag to remove residual dirt and moisture. Work on the axle until all reachable parts are clean. This includes the outer ring where spokes are attached. In tight spots, such as the recessed holes where the ends of the spokes protrude, use a toothbrush as necessary.

Work your way out from the hub, taking time to clean each spoke out to the rim. This is where a sock or small cloth is handy. Spokes still soiled with road film are cleaned by spraying cleaner on a

The majority of cleaning work has already been done to this rear wheel assembly. Detailed cleaning includes removing the rings of grease from sprocket teeth, and detail work to the hub.

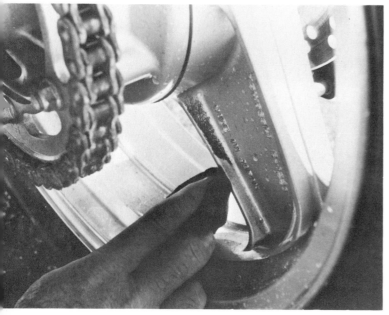

Small spots of dirt and grease build-up on wheels are an eyesore. Definitive cleaning ensures that these nuisance items are properly removed.

Chrome-spoked wheels present detailers with lots of small corners and crevices to clean. Take time to remove dirt from the base of nipples and the threads on rim locks.

Spoked wheels are designed in such a way that access to the hub is limited. Art Wentworth has had good luck buffing hubs as opposed to wiping them. This works well for drying and for removing polish and wax.

cloth first and then wiping. Spraying cleaner directly on the spoke will result in overspray on the rest of the wheel, an unnecessary mess.

Pay attention to the pattern you have chosen to use. You want to be sure to clean each spoke, but there is no reason to clean them more than once. From one side of the wheel, you should be able to reach through the spokes to get at those that are attached to the other side of the hub. If not, position yourself at the front of the wheel with the tire against your chest. One hand can clean the right side, the other the left.

At the rim, use a toothbrush to clean nipples and the surrounding surface. Don't forget to clean the valve stem and its cap, as well as rim lock stems and nuts. A toothbrush works well to clean the grooves in valve stem caps and threads on rim lock stems. Move along the rim until you come to the next spoke. Clean the base and then work your way back to the hub. The pattern is simple. Clean outward on one spoke, and then inward on the next. This allows continuity with no wasted motion.

As you move around the wheel, you will come up against obstacles such as forks, swing arms and shock absorbers. To keep your place while turning the wheel, place your cleaning cloth between the last spoke cleaned and the next in line. Tie a piece of string or a shred of rag around the starting spoke to mark the place where work began. You can also start at the valve stem, using it as a starting and ending point.

While cleaning, note any loose spokes. You may not want to tighten them right away, as there may be quite a few, and uneven tightening will cause the wheel to be out of round. Mark loose spokes with a string or piece of masking tape.

When the entire wheel has been cleaned and loose spokes marked, you can make necessary adjustments.

Ralph Maughn pulls the entire wheel off of his bike when too many spokes are loose. He places the wheel on a stand he made, which supports the wheel on its axle. After each spoke is tightened, the wheel is spun to ensure that it is true. While the wheel spins, he focuses his eyes on one spot at the edge of the rim and aligns it with a projection or corner of the stand. Any wobble in the rim is easily noticed and corrective spoke adjustment made. By going slowly and checking the rim after adjusting each spoke, Maughn has been able to keep the chrome-spoked wheels on his bike in good operating condition.

Polishing chrome spokes and rims presents no special problem, with the exception of access. You will have to be patient and inventive. Once again, an old sock may work best, since it will stay in place on your hand and not get caught up in the

Dan Mycon's Sportster has chrome-spoked wheels. They are maintained in excellent condition. To remove dirt build-up from nipples on clean rims, he uses the soft scrub of a toothbrush.

Neglected spokes may require more cleaning power than is provided with cleaner and a towel. Here, dirty spokes are cleaned with the light touch of an SOS pad.

other spokes. Ordinary chrome polish is fine, Happich Simichrome, Eagle 1 Mag & Chrome Polish and Mother's all work well too. Spokes in good shape with no rust showing and plenty of shine may not need polishing, just a light coat of wax.

Rust deposits on the threads at the rim end of spokes need polishing. If the cloth does not reach into these small grooves, apply polish to the threads with your finger and then work it in with a cotton swab. This is meticulous work, to say the least. You may also use the "shoe shine" method by placing a small, thin cloth around the spoke, holding an end in each hand, with the spoke in the middle of the cloth. Move your hands back and forth to buff the spoke.

Polish the rim as necessary. Avoid smearing polish on the tire and valve stem. Use a clean sock on your other hand to buff off excess polish and any film that may have developed. If a small cloth is used, buff with a clean section after polishing.

After the entire assembly has been polished, you should apply a light coat of protective wax. Meguiar's Hi-Tech Yellow Wax #26 or other carnauba-based wax offers the longest lasting protection. Liquid or paste wax can be used, depending upon your preference. Application is the same as for polish. Again, don't be in a hurry, and avoid smearing tires and packing excess wax on nipples and recessed areas on the hub. Buff off dried wax with a soft cloth and use the cut-off paintbrush as necessary.

Painted spoked wheels

These wheels are cleaned just like chrome-spoked wheels. Instead of using chrome polish, use a glaze to brighten dull or oxidized spokes and rims. Afterward, apply a light coat of carnauba wax to keep the rejuvenated paint looking good.

Many enthusiasts prefer to use a one-step cleaner wax on painted wheels. This is because they can polish and wax in one operation. Art Wentworth has had good luck using Meguiar's Car

Sometimes, no cleaning tool works as well as your fingers. Many times, Art Wentworth simply wipes dirty spots with his fingers to quickly remove light dirt film. Use caution though, especially near sharp points—you don't want to damage these tools.

Riding motorcycles in the dirt is hard on wheels. To keep his wheels true, Ralph Maughn built this wheel holder, which allows him to spin the wheel and check for roundness while tightening spokes. After each spoke is tightened, the wheel is spun and Maughn focuses on the edge of the rim to see that it stays in line with a solid point on the stand.

Cleaner Wax. It works well and in many cases removes oxidation and dullness with just one application. The wax protection may not last as long as a carnauba-based wax, but the ease of application may be worth a more frequent application schedule.

Quite often, painted wheels become chipped and severely scratched. No amount of polishing will remove the blemish. In those instances, you may have to do some touch-up paint work. Touch-up paint in just the right color may be hard to find, since most bikes with painted spokes, hubs and rims are quite old. To match paint, bring the bike to an auto body paint and supply store. The folks at these stores are quite knowledgeable and can match just about any color you present them with.

Paint application is made with a fine artist's paintbrush. An assortment of artist's brushes is found at most stationery and craft stores, as well as artist supply shops. Rest your hand against the wheel while applying paint. This will help you steady the brush and put paint on the chip or scratch with little trouble. After paint has had ample time to cure, generally about a week, use polishing compound to smooth rough edges. Follow that with an application of sealer/glaze and then carnauba. The wheel will look stunning.

Alloy wheels

Mag wheels are not nearly as labor intensive to clean as spoked styles. Detailed cleaning requires the same sort of concentration, but with far fewer intricate pieces to contend with. A paintbrush and toothbrush will serve you well, especially in styles featuring long grooves and ridges running lengthwise along the separate spoke braces.

Simple Green sprayed or dabbed on a clean cloth will quickly remove dirt and grease build-up missed on the wash rack. Consider using a cloth dampened with clear water to wipe off residue left behind by the cleaning cloth. This will ensure a perfectly clean surface before the application of wax.

Bare alloy

Bare alloy wheels are polished and then waxed to seal metal and prevent oxidation. Be absolutely certain, though, that the wheels on your bike are bare metal and not clear-coated. Mag and Chrome Polish will ruin a clear-coat finish. You should be able to feel the difference between the two. Clear-coated wheels are velvety smooth to the touch, while bare wheels are rather rough in comparison. If you have the slightest doubt, hop on the bike and ride it to the closest motorcycle shop. The

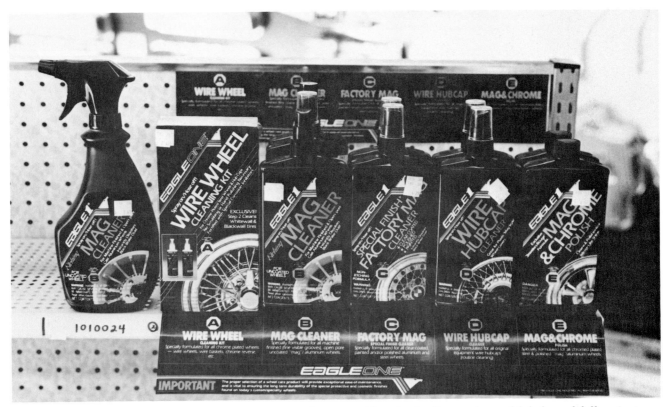

Eagle 1 offers probably the widest variety of chemical wheel cleaners. Their Uniform Wheel Care System clearly identifies which products are to be used on spe- *cific wheels. Be sure to read labels and follow instructions.*

folks at the shop will be glad to show you the difference between bare and clear-coated wheels.

Polishing is done with any brand of mag polish you choose to use. Most work quite well, although many motorcycle enthusiasts and shop owners seem to have their own preference. Harley-Davidson owners like Mother's, BMW riders have had good luck with Ouator, Suzuki fans have used Eagle 1 with success and some Honda enthusiasts prefer Simichrome. You will just have to try them all until you find the one that works best on your bike.

Application of polish is the same as for any type of surface needing a shine. Use sparingly, as a little goes a long way. Do a little at a time, maybe six inches at a stretch. Follow the directions on the label to achieve optimum results.

When the wheel is polished to its brightest, apply a light coat of wax. This will help the wheel to shed road grime and prevent minute deposits of dirt from becoming embedded in the metal grain, causing stains. Again, too much is not good. Apply wax with a soft cloth or damp sponge. Then buff off dry wax with a soft clean cloth.

Clear-coated alloy

A clear-coated wheel has a layer of clear lacquer paint applied over the surface of bare metal. Paint protects the metal from corrosion and dirt. Like the paint on a fuel tank, it is susceptible to scratching. To remove minor scratches and blemishes from clear coats, use a polish designed for them.

Meguiar's manufactures a number of products specifically designed for clear-coat finishes. Their

The rear tire on Squire Tomasie's ZX-10 sports a definite ridge. Dressing should never be applied over the ridge into tread. This type of sidewall ridge is quite common on road bike tires.

Professional Hi-Tech Cleaner #2 is designed to remove oxidation, harsh scratches and swirls. Professional Hi-Tech Swirl Remover #9 is less abrasive and will leave the surface satiny smooth and swirl-free. Meguiar's recommends any application of their #2 or #9 be followed with Hi-Tech Yellow Wax #26 for maximum gloss retention and protection.

Be sure to read the label on any product you plan to apply on a clear-coated piece of equipment. Not every polish or wax is compatible with clear-coat paints. Some may be too abrasive and cause unnecessary scratching, while others may be too weak and show no improvement whatsoever.

Special wheels

Keen competition among motorcycle manufacturers has been a boon to motorcycle enthusiasts. We have seen a new breed of motorcycle hit the streets in the last few years, and it has caused a great deal of excitement. Part of this innovation has taken place with the advent of special wheels. Their styles and colors vary a great deal.

Barney Li, owner of Eagle 1 Industries, has spent a lot of money, time and effort to devise a Uniform Wheel Care System for automobile wheels. He recognized the influx of new wheels, and the need for specific products to clean and shine particular brands and styles. This same concern can be shared by many motorcycle enthusiasts.

Since there are so many different types of wheels for motorcycles, it is best to check with the motorcycle dealer to determine which product is best suited for cleaning and polishing the wheels on your bike. Harsh cleaners may etch those peculiar wheels featuring soft metal, and certain polishing products may cause undue wear. You should never go wrong using mild soap and a soft paintbrush for cleaning. Polish and wax products should be confirmed safe by a knowledgeable expert before application.

Tire cleaning

A comprehensive detailing includes attention to the tires as well as the rims. Cleaning the tires allows you to carefully inspect them for sidewall cracks and worn tread. And proper dressing of your tires will make them look new again.

Cleaning

Scrubbing tires with soap and water and a plastic brush generally leaves them looking new. Detailed cleaning will ensure their like-new appearance and give you a chance to inspect the condition of the tread and sidewalls.

A slightly damp SOS pad will remove minor blemishes left on whitewalls. Persistent stains on whitewalls or blackwalls will have to be scrubbed with an SOS pad or whitewall brush. Use a toothbrush to remove lingering debris in tread, sidewall lettering and the tight groove next to the rim. New tires are sometimes dotted with manufacturer stamps that are easily wiped away with a dab of solvent on a clean rag.

Aggressive tire cleaning will spot wheels with soapsuds and cleaner residue. On the other hand, aggressive wheel cleaning will surely result in some spotting of tires. The best bet is to clean as thoroughly as possible during the initial wash, leaving only minor chores to detailed cleaning.

The choice between cleaning the wheel or tire first is up to you. Art Wentworth likes to get the dirtiest jobs done first, on the theory that detailed cleaning will not result in much residue. If the initial wash failed to clean the wheel or tire sufficiently, I recommend you pull the bike back out to the driveway and go at it again with cleaner and brushes and plenty of clear water for rinsing.

Dressing

Too much tire dressing applied to motorcycle tires can be dangerous. Because polypenetrants make rubber and vinyl surfaces slippery, you should be concerned about slippery side treads when riding around corners. It is best to apply a minimal amount of dressing on the solid sidewall only, leaving all tread bare.

Controlled application on a clean surface is a must. Rory Vance, Art Wentworth and Bill Buckingham apply dressing to a cloth first and then carefully wipe it on the sidewall. Sport bikes feature a raised ridge between the tread and sidewall, which makes a perfect stopping point for dressing application. Other tires may have a line or other mark between the tread and sidewall which you can use as a guide.

Dan Mycon does not use dressing and prefers to leave tires clean and bare. His Sportster is frequently washed and is always parked under a clean cotton motorcycle cover.

Armor All is a favorite of Wentworth's while Vance likes Turtle Wax Clear Guard. Buckingham has had good luck with Meguiar's #40 and Ralph Maughn uses them all. It is hard to get motorcycle enthusiasts to agree on any one product, but easy to note their common belief that improper dressing application can be a definite riding hazard.

Even with slow and controlled dressing application, smears on rims are not uncommon. Wipe them off with a clean cloth. Blue tints left behind on whitewalls are quickly removed with a dry edge of an SOS pad. Accidental smudges on tire treads should be removed right away with cleaner and a cloth.

As with all detail work involving wheels and tires, the wheel will have to be rotated, or the bike moved, in order to gain access to all parts of the sidewall for dressing. Dress both sides of the tire before moving the bike or spinning the wheel.

Unique designs on sidewalls may make it difficult for a dressing cloth to apply dressing next to prominent ridges featured on recessed and raised lettering. To achieve complete coverage in these tight spots, use a clean paintbrush to work in dressing. A light spray of dressing on the bristles of a thin brush is all that is needed for adequate and thorough coverage.

Tire dressing looks best, according to many enthusiasts, when it has been lightly applied, adequately worked into the surface and excess thoroughly buffed off. In other words, these folks do not appreciate excessive gloss. They prefer a tire that looks new and clean, not wet and slippery. In this case, too much is not good—nor is it safe.

Chain and sprocket

Chains and sprockets collect more dirt, grime and grease than any other type of drive. The chain lube is flung from the chain onto the swing arm, chain guard, wheel and fender where it acts as a magnet for any dirt in the area. Most of the big areas

Ralph Maughn is holding the chain from his Yamaha before soaking it in kerosene. Chains should hang loosely and wriggle freely when held like this. The wide notch on the right side of the chain shows it is stiff from caked-on dirt and grime—not a good sign.

79

should have been cleaned during the initial wash. Detailing this area consists of cleaning and lubing the chain and cleaning the sprockets.

Cleaning chains

Optimal chain cleaning is done with it off the bike. Fill a large pan, like an oil drain pan, with kerosene. Lay the chain in the pan of kerosene and allow it to soak for a while, at least a half an hour. Use a parts brush or old paintbrush to work kerosene in and grime out. Empty the pan as the liquid becomes extra dirty and refill with fresh kerosene. When you are satisfied with the results, lay the chain on an old towel and dry. Then, hang it up and let it drip dry for an hour. Be sure to place a large rag under it to catch drips.

The chain will look dry and faded when all of the kerosene has dissipated. It will need total lubrication.

If the chain is on the bike, you will have to use a towel dampened with kerosene to wipe off the chain. You will not be able to remove all of the grit trapped inside, but you should certainly be able to clean the outer sides. Do *not* hold on to the chain and spin the rear wheel to get the job done quicker. It is far too easy to catch fingers between the chain and sprocket. Hold the wheel still, and move your hand back and forth on the chain.

O-ring chains require cleaning with a mild product like kerosene. WD-40 works fine but doesn't last long. Other harsh solvents wear down the soft rubber O-rings. If you are in doubt as to the best cleaning product to use on your chain, check with a local motorcycle shop.

Lubricating chains

Every enthusiast has a favorite method and product for lubricating the chain. Ralph Maughn likes Lith-Ease white lithium grease. He applies it often and is pleased with the minimal amount of dirt and grime it collects. After letting the chain from his Yamaha TT 600 K sit in kerosene for a week, Ralph let it dry and then soaked it in a pan of fresh motor oil for another week. After wiping off excess oil, he replaced the chain on the bike, and then applied Lith-Ease.

To minimize the amount of dirt that clings to his chain, Wally Shearer always uses WD-40. He says that the lubricant does a good job of cleaning as well as lubricating. Since it doesn't seem to last long, he applies it to the chain on his dirt bike after every motocross heat, most of which take about twenty minutes to complete. He goes on to say that frequent applications also clean the chain, thus reducing grime build-up and premature wear. This combination is great for motocross because the surface is generally sandy and the length of each ride is short.

Dan Mycon uses Harley-Davidson chain lube on his Sportster, while Art Wentworth believes in using whatever product the manufacturer recommends. His solution to reducing chain lube build-up is frequent soap and water washing.

Cleaning sprockets

If the chain is removed, cleaning the sprockets is much easier. Simply wipe off any remaining

The stiff and dirty chain from Maughn's Yamaha was allowed to soak in a tub of kerosene for a week. Periodically an old paintbrush was used to agitate debris from inside the links. Note the air cleaner at the bottom. It was cleaned, and serviced with air cleaner oil at the same time.

Further maintenance of Maughn's chain was accomplished by letting it soak in a tub of fresh motor oil for a week. After it was put back on the bike, actual chain lube was applied.

grease or dirt with a dampened rag. Wipe the entire sprocket, including the face and center section next to the axle. Use a toothbrush, as necessary, to remove any build-up around bolts.

If the chain is not removed, you will have to wipe around it, as well as you can. This job is made easier if the rear wheel is off the ground and can spin freely. Use extreme caution, as fingers can quickly and painfully get caught between the chain and the sprocket.

To clean the outer ring of the sprocket, drape a cloth over your hand and dampen the area above your thumb and forefinger with kerosene. Then, pinch the sprocket on the open space between the chain links and rub the grease away. When that part is clean, move your hand and spin the wheel until a dirty section fills the space. Leftover grease smears are wiped off with cleaner.

Wipe the entire sprocket, including the face and center section next to the axle. Then use a toothbrush as necessary to remove any build-up around bolts.

Belt drives

Belt drives are simple and present little area to clean. Most of the time, only the top surface needs to be cleaned. This is done with a cloth and mild cleaner, using a paintbrush or toothbrush for stubborn stains.

Periodically, especially after riding on wet pavement or a gravel road, you should take time to clean the bottom side of the belt as well as the valleys on the sprockets. Grit tends to build up in these areas after being thrown up by the rear tire. Grit acts as an abrasive and will grind against the belt to a point where it may snap.

In order to reach the belt, you may have to remove the belt guard attached to the swing arm. This will allow much better access for a small paintbrush or toothbrush. If your bike features only a side stand, you will have to roll it forward or backward a little at a time to expose all parts of the belt and sprocket.

The rear sprocket is equally difficult to reach for cleaning and polishing. You will need patience and do just a small portion at a time. Then, roll the bike forward to gain access to another section. Since the space around the sprocket is so tight, polishing with a sponge is impractical. Instead, place your finger inside a small clean cloth to apply and wipe off polish. You can further protect the sprocket by applying a light coat of wax after pol-

Stubborn dirt deposits on brake assemblies are quickly removed with a paintbrush and toothbrush. Pay close attention to the areas surrounding screws, bolts and fittings.

ishing. Polish and wax residue caught in valleys and around obstacles is removed with the cut-off paintbrush.

Brakes

Motorcycle brake assembly detailing ranges from a simple cleaning with a paintbrush and toothbrush, to an in-depth dismantling and individual part refurbishing. It depends on the overall condition of the motorcycle. If a bike with drum brakes has spent years in storage, an entire season in the dirt, or has just completed a cross-country trip, it is a good idea to pull the wheels and visually inspect the drums and shoes.

Disc brake models present other unique detailing chores. Rusted cast iron discs must be removed for cleaning. Other discs feature holes and slots where dirt, grit and brake dust accumulate. Caliper housing designs generally have grooves and valleys where the same kind of debris builds up. Patient detail work with a paintbrush and toothbrush will remove stubborn deposits and help those parts look their best.

Disc brakes

Disc brake calipers and assemblies are not hard to detail. During the initial wash, plenty of scrubbing with the paintbrush and toothbrush should have removed almost all build-up accumulations. Remaining spots are quickly cleaned with a toothbrush and small cloth.

Discs

The holes so frequently found on brake discs do accumulate some build-up. Dirt that is not removed from the small holes with brushes is cleaned with cotton swabs. Be sure to clean the outer edge of the disc too.

The inside face of the disc is tough to reach. The best time to clean this part is during the initial wash, with lots of soap and water and a small paintbrush and toothbrush. Detailed cleaning is achieved by reaching through the spokes with a small cloth and reaching down the side of the disc with your hand in a clean sock. Extra-stubborn build-up is lightly buffed with #0000 steel wool or an SOS pad. A soft touch is necessary to prevent scratching.

It is not uncommon for brake discs to warp. Repair is made easiest by purchasing and installing a new disc. There are a few machine shops that can resurface motorcycle brake discs and you will have to determine if it is more cost effective to have it resurfaced or replaced.

After a long trip in the desert or a riding season in the hills, it is a good idea to check the condition of brake shoes and drums. Dust and grit inside the hub will cause wear and possible brake damage.

Some bikes are equipped with cast iron brake discs. The brake pads keep most of the disc shiny while untouched sections are susceptible to rust. The best way to combat this problem is to remove the disc, treat corrosion with Naval Jelly and then paint those areas which are not contacted by the brake pads.

Steve Giblin is the Service Manager for Dewey's Cycle in Seattle. His shop mainly deals with English bikes like BSA and Triumph. Quite often, he must restore neglected cast iron discs for installation onto a vintage bike. He has had good luck using Naval Jelly and Metal Prep to remove rust, and also found that sandblasting does a fine job. After the disc has been properly cleaned, he uses heat resistant paint to cover those areas of the disc that will not be touched by the brake pads to protect them from future rust problems. Heat-resistant paint must be used, as ordinary paint will not stand up under the high temperatures frequently encountered during brake usage.

Calipers

Brake caliper housings are either bare or painted. If detailed cleaning with a toothbrush reveals the paint is chipped or peeling, it may be best to pull it off the bike for sanding and painting. Use folds in #600 wet-and-dry sandpaper to reach into valleys and seams for smoothing paint chips. Mask carefully and apply two to three light coats as op-

posed to a single heavy coat. Follow the instructions on the paint can as to drying time between coats.

Bare calipers are subject to fading. You can polish them with a mild polish and a toothbrush. Some enthusiasts have used chemical mag wheel cleaners with good results, but they run the risk of damaging the calipers by using an incorrect product. This is especially true if the caliper housing has been clear coated. Clear-coated parts require polish and cleaners designed just for them. It is best to stay with gentle methods and mild products. Read the label on various polish containers to see if they are designed for use on clear-coated parts.

Drum brakes

After his extended Baja trip, Ralph Maughn removed the wheels from his Yamaha TT 600 K for cleaning. At the same time, he checked the condition of the drum brakes.

Tiny particles of grit and sand can quickly damage brake shoes and drums. Use a dry paintbrush to dislodge particles and whisk away debris. Further repairs can be made as necessary, such as sanding off the glaze from brake shoes with sandpaper.

Glaze on brake shoes is removed with light sanding using #400 wet-and-dry sandpaper. Ralph Maughn was surprised at the better-than-average condition of the brakes on his Yamaha after the Baja trip. It's probably because he didn't use them much.

To clean and shine the bare aluminum brake housing on this BSA front wheel, Steve Giblin will use a paintbrush and a mild solution of Alumiprep. This product is very potent and must be diluted with two to three parts water. It is found at auto body paint and supply stores and will remove oxidation, not grease or dirt.

Chapter 6

Frame, suspension and stands

Motorcycle frame detailing is as varied as the machines themselves. Dirt bikes generally sport a frame that is highly visible and easy to detail. Touring bikes, loaded with saddlebags, full fairings and fenders, almost cover the frame completely. Sport bike designs intertwine the frame with wraparound fairings and it is hard to tell which is which.

Forks are a different story. Again, they are plainly out in the open on dirt bikes, and hidden to various degrees on road machines. Fairings, fenders and headlight assemblies are engineered around forks, making it hard to reach some sections for detailing.

Kickstands are tucked under the motorcycle out of sight in the up position, but are almost always plainly accessible when down. Center and side stand detailing poses no special problems, it is just a matter of getting down on the ground and doing it.

Detailing these parts of a motorcycle includes definitive cleaning, polishing, waxing and some touch-up paint work. If the frame, painted fork sec-

Areas under the seat and fuel tank become quite dusty. Work with a paintbrush and damp cloth to clean the frame, wires and other accessories located in this space.

tions or kickstand on your machine suffer a multitude of paint chips or heavy scratches, the correct color of touch-up paint should be purchased from the dealer before the project is started.

Frame

Steve Jacobs has owned his 1978 Suzuki RM 250 since new. Every couple of years, he gets ambitious and dismantles the bike down to the frame. He uses a small floor jack to support the engine during its removal. The engine is light enough so that Jacobs can lift it onto a workbench for detailed cleaning, and all nuts and bolts are put into a can of solvent to loosen up grease and grime. He also removes and details the forks, shocks, wiring, hand controls and so on. Left with virtually a bare frame, he then cleans and paints as necessary.

This may be a great winter project for Jacobs and Ralph Maughn on their dirt bikes, but a major undertaking for Don Perry and his Gold Wing Interstate. You have to determine just how far to go with frame detailing on your motorcycle.

Cleaning

Removing the seat and fuel tank (storage box in the case of Perry's Gold Wing) is a necessity. This gives you access to the top of the frame and wiring harness that runs along it. You will be surprised at how much dust and dirt accumulate on this part of the frame. Be sure to turn off the fuel valve at the bottom of the fuel tank before you take it off the bike. Place the tank on a piece of cardboard or a large towel so it does not get scratched.

Removing the tank is also necessary, in many cases, to allow access to the top of the engine and carburetors. Mechanics have to remove tanks in order to reach the top of the engine for valve and carburetor adjustment on some sport and touring machines. If you anticipate the tank will have to be removed for service or detailing, plan ahead so that there is a minimal amount of fuel in the tank. A smaller fuel load makes the overall tank lighter and easier to handle.

To protect the top of a clean engine, lay a towel or cloth on top of it to catch dirt debris and cleaner residue. Light dusting is done with a damp towel. Dust and dirt build-up is dislodged with a paintbrush or toothbrush. For spots with high concentrations of build-up, spray the bristles of a paintbrush with cleaner and agitate. Then wipe off with a towel.

Starting at the front of the frame next to the triple clamp, work your way back to the rear. Take your time and move wires as needed to clean the frame under them. Don't overlook dirty wires.

A pre-planned, systematic approach will fare-you-well. Along with the fuel tank, the seat should be off of the bike. This allows access to the frame under it. Inch by inch, every part of the frame needs to be cleaned, including top, sides and bottom. Box-type frames feature more surface area than tubular models. They also include more gussets,

Battery brackets are frequently overlooked during a wash and wax. While performing an annual detail, remove batteries and check brackets. Many times, they are dirty and show signs of corrosion. Clean, sand and paint as necessary.

A paintbrush and towel quickly clean the tops of batteries and the surrounding surface areas to make them look crisp. While working in this area, check the water level in batteries and the condition of terminals.

Brisk agitation with a paintbrush will remove dust build-up from around battery caps. Wentworth has tidily coiled the vest warmer wire and secured it with a wide rubber band.

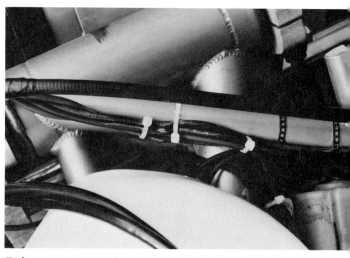

Ridges, common along welds, collect dirt and dust build-up. If a paintbrush is not stout enough to remove dirt, use a toothbrush. You can see how plastic wire clamps keep wires in an orderly position.

which need cleaning next to ridges and welds. A toothbrush works very well to dislodge stubborn dirt and grime from those ridges commonly found around welds.

If you should happen across a particularly greasy part of frame, use solvent or Gunk on a paper towel to remove the large portion of grease. Follow up with another application to wipe away remaining smears. Then, wash that part again with a degreasing cleaner like Simple Green. Cleaner re-

moves the petroleum-based film left behind by solvent. This is necessary because solvent residue will cause touch-up paint to run and not set properly. On some pieces, especially around the engine, you may have to scrub the frame with an SOS pad and wipe with paint thinner to remove this greasy film and give paint a clean base.

Painting

With all the parts taken off, Steve Jacobs has little trouble painting the bare frame on his Suzuki.

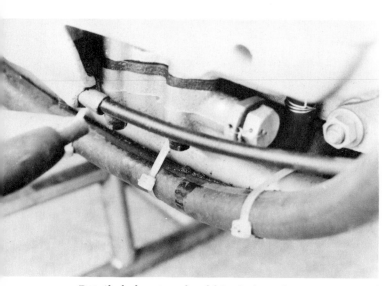

Detailed cleaning should include a close inspection of wires and hoses running along the frame. This accumulation of grime is removed with a paintbrush and rag. Don't forget to clean the underside of hoses and wires.

Greasy spots found along the frame and lower parts of the bike are cleaned with a dab of solvent on a paper towel or rag. This shift lever should be removed for detailed cleaning and painting. Shift and brake levers are commonly located together on the right side of flat-track race bikes.

Preliminary work includes thorough cleaning and some sanding. When a complete paint job is called for, he likes to sand the entire frame with #600 wet-and-dry sandpaper. This takes the gloss off and gives paint a good base. Severe scratches may have to be sanded with a coarser sandpaper first, to knock down ridges and smooth the overall area. Fine sanding with #600 sandpaper removes lines left by the previous sanding, leaving the base extra smooth.

When sanding has brought the surface down to bare metal, it is a good idea to apply a light coat of primer. Again, this serves as a good base for paint. If primer runs, use #600 wet-and-dry sandpaper to smooth. Read the label on the can of primer to determine drying time before sanding or paint application.

Masking should be minimal on a bare frame. You may want to protect parts around the triple clamp and swing arm hinge points. Additional masking will be needed on any item you want to remain unpainted, such as manufacturer labels, off-road permits and so forth. Masking tape is easy to apply and remove. Take your time and be sure tape covers all of the surface you want it to, especially around the outer edges of the item being masked.

Spray paint seems to go on and adhere much better in warm temperatures. To help the process, warm the can of spray paint in a sink of warm water. Warm water is designated as water that is not too hot for your hand. Never place an aerosol can in a pot of water on the stove to heat it up. Excessive temperatures can cause the can to explode. Warning labels on spray paint cans advise against subjecting the contents to over 120 degrees Fahrenheit.

Follow the application instructions on the label of paint you have chosen to use. Gloss and semi-gloss black are popular choices for most dirt bikes with tubular black frames. These paints are readily available at auto parts stores. You will have to read the labels to see which brand offers the most advantages for the job you are doing. Other stock colors can be purchased at a motorcycle shop to ensure the correct tint. If they are not available at the bike shop, have an auto body paint and supply store match the color for you.

Complete frame painting is easiest on dirt bikes because they are not loaded with extra equipment and huge engines. Painting the frame on a Gold Wing or Electra Glide is a different story, however. First, frames on street motorcycles do not suffer nearly the amount or severity of paint chips and scratches dirt bikes do. Second, dismantling a loaded street bike is a major undertaking. There are numerous accessories to remove and the engines are generally much too heavy to easily lift out of the frame.

It is doubtful you should ever have to completely repaint the frame on a street motorcycle. More than likely, this breed of bike will need periodic touch-up on exposed frame members behind the front wheel, and along lower parts susceptible to rock chips.

Touch-up paint in little bottles with a brush attached to the cap are available at most motorcycle shops. Various colors are displayed to help you match the color of your motorcycle's frame.

Application is simple. Follow the instructions on the label and be sure the area around the paint chip is clean. Use a dab of Prepsol or paint thinner as necessary to remove any hint of grease or road oil. Shake the bottle vigorously before opening.

As you pull off the cap, slide the brush over the edge of the bottle to force excess paint off of the bristles. To steady your hand while painting, lean it against the bike and let your fingers do the work. Apply paint in thin coats. Allow each coat to dry before applying the second and successive coats.

In cooler weather, cans of spray paint are warmed in a sink of warm water (water should not be too hot for your hand). This thins paint and activates all the potential of internal propellants. Never subject spray cans to temperatures of 120 degrees or over, as per label instructions.

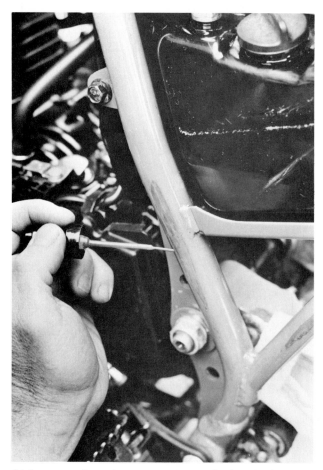

Light coats of touch-up paint are applied to the frame of Ralph Maughn's Yamaha. Rest your hand against part of the bike for support, while applying paint in a steady and controlled fashion. The brush used here is attached to the cap from a bottle of touch-up paint. The particular color was purchased at a Yamaha shop.

In the down position, center stands are easy to clean and detail. You will have to get down on the ground, and may consider lying on a tarp or drop cloth.

When the touch-up has had plenty of time to dry, according to label instructions, you should use polishing compound to smooth the surface and help it blend even better with the surrounding surface. After that, polish with a fine sealer/glaze like Meguiar's #7 to remove light scratches left behind. Finally, wax the entire polished area with a light coat of carnauba wax for long-lasting protection.

If touch-up work has not turned out as smooth as you would like, sand the spot with #600 or finer wet-and-dry sandpaper. To protect surrounding paint, mask the spot with masking tape. This will ensure that only the touched-up spot gets sanded, since masking tape will be covering the frame surrounding the spot. Lightly sand until the blemish is smooth. Follow sanding with an application or two of polishing compound. Then remove the masking tape and polish with a sealer/glaze and wax with carnauba.

Kickstand and center stand

Definitive center and side stand cleaning is not a big chore. Most of the time, a little attention during the initial wash is sufficient. For that once-a-year detail, though, it is always a good idea to get on the ground and thoroughly clean, lubricate and paint these items.

Cleaning

Kickstand cleaning falls right in line with frame cleaning. Clean the kickstands as you come to them during frame cleaning. You will be on the ground cleaning lower frame members anyway, and your cleaning tools will be close at hand.

Use a paintbrush and toothbrush as necessary. A damp SOS pad may come in handy for extra-stubborn dirt deposits and stains. Be sure to clean springs and around nuts, bolts and hinge points as well.

Skid plates are another item that should be considered during detailed cleaning. The bottom is not much of a problem. The top, however, collects a lot of dirt, grease and grime. Since most skid plates are held on by only a few bolts, it is best to remove them for cleaning and painting.

Painting

Kickstands are touched up on the bike with spray paint, as long as surrounding parts are protected from overspray. Use newspaper and masking tape as necessary. Be sure to cover the garage floor or driveway with newspaper to protect it from overspray.

The best way to paint kickstands is off of the motorcycle. Lighter bikes are supported on a crate or other makeshift support while the kickstand is removed. Clean, sand and prime as needed.

An old coat hanger works great as a hook. Open it up and place one end through an opening on the kickstand. Hang the other end from a nail or other support at a location where overspray will not cause a problem, like a rafter close to the garage door opening. With the kickstand hanging freely, you can paint the entire part thoroughly. This same procedure works very well for skid plates too.

Dull and chipped kickstand bolt heads should also be painted so they don't stand out like a sore thumb next to a freshly painted kickstand. Poke a hole in a piece of cardboard and insert the bolt through it. The cardboard supports the bolt in an upright position during painting, allowing access to its entire head surface and all sides. It also serves as protection against overspray.

Small paint chips on the frame and kickstand can be touched up individually without the use of the brush from a bottle of touch-up paint. If all you have is a can of matching spray paint and don't want to spray the entire part, or, if the can of paint you have doesn't have a brush, use a paper matchstick or fine artist's paintbrush.

For years, motorcycle enthusiasts have used the bottom end of a paper matchstick to apply paint to chips and nicks. Although somewhat primitive, it has been done successfully thousands of times. Simply dip the end of the matchstick in the paint and apply as you would with the special bottle cap brush.

A far better application is made using a fine artist's paintbrush. These brushes are commonly found in stationery stores and artist supply and hobby shops. After the brush has been used, clean it and apply a light coat of petroleum jelly to the bristles. This helps to keep them straight, protected and in their original shape.

If a spray can is the only supply of matching paint you have, and you don't want to spray the part needing paint, spray a puddle of paint onto a piece of cardboard. Just hold the nozzle in one spot and allow paint to puddle. You don't need a lot, just enough to dip a matchstick or artist's brush into for paint retrieval.

To keep nozzles on cans of spray paint in working order, you have to clear them at the end of each use. Simply turn the can upside down and activate the nozzle. A slight amount of paint will come out, so watch where the nozzle is aimed. When the nozzle tube is empty of paint, clear propellent will be ejected. As soon as you notice this, stop. The nozzle and feeding tube have been cleared and should be clean. Wipe off excess paint drops from the tip of the nozzle with a rag dabbed in thinner.

Front suspension

Front suspension detailing consists of cleaning, polishing and touching up the paint on the forks and triple clamp assemblies. On most bikes, these parts are in the open and easy to detail.

Side stands present no unusual cleaning problems. Use a toothbrush to remove dirt and grease from the hinge point, spring and supporting nut and bolt. After cleaning, lubricate the joint.

Side stands can be painted any color you choose. Painting them on top of newspaper or cardboard will require two sessions; the bottom side cannot be painted until the top is dry. It is better to suspend these pieces from hooks, which allows the entire unit to be painted in one shot.

Fork cleaning

Definitive cleaning of the forks includes all of the processes discussed so far. The same tools and cleaners are used, as well as the same meticulous care and concentration to detail. Special cleaning attention should be given to that part of the individual fork that slides into the other. Basically designed as a two-piece assembly, the upper fork portion attached to the triple clamp is rigid. The lower section moves with the front wheel and slides over the top section as the wheel hits a bump. Fork fluid and springs are compressed inside the fork tubes, which gives the forks their shock absorption ability.

Fork tubes pass through a seal at the top of the bottom section. The seal is designed to keep fork fluid inside the forks. If hardened bug residue or other debris is allowed to remain on fork tubes, these seals will be damaged.

Ralph Maughn's Yamaha features a flexible boot over the fork tubes. Harley-Davidson Electra Glides sport a solid shield over theirs, and other bikes offer protection by way of wraparound fairings. Concern over hardened debris on the tubes of

The front forks on this Electra Glide are out in the open and easy to clean. This front wheel assembly is crisp looking and tidy. Note the clear definition and uniform shine on all parts.

Fork seals can be damaged by hardened residue stuck on the tubes. The clamp on this seal should be removed, cleaned, sanded and painted to make it look new.

90

these models is negligible. On other bikes, though, where forks are out in the open and unprotected, this should be a fundamental concern.

The best way to prevent debris from hardening on the forks is to maintain a frequent washing schedule. Aside from that, you may have to use an SOS pad or light application of #0000 steel wool and wax to remove the problem. The bare metal part of fork tubes is shined with chrome polish and protected with a light coat of wax. Art Wentworth likes to apply Meguiar's Car Cleaner Wax to this part on his Suzuki. He believes that this not only helps to keep forks clean and looking good, but also helps to keep them smooth, so they are gentle on seals.

Rubber fork tube protection boots are cleaned as necessary with cleaner, a cloth and a paintbrush. They can be removed and cleaned with soap and water in the sink, but that would entail removing the forks. The decision to remove and clean is up to you and the condition of the boots. When cleaning and drying is complete, a light coat of Armor All or other dressing will help the boots to look new.

Fork painting

The bottom part of front forks are generally painted. Cleaning, polishing and waxing proce-

The lower forks on SquireTomasie's flat-track bikes are constantly pelted by track debris. This piece must be sanded and painted to look new again.

dures are no different than for other painted parts. Because this area of the motorcycle is virtually unprotected from road hazards, paint chips are a common problem. Repairing paint chips entails the same methods as described for frame touch-up.

Use the buffing method with a towel to clean and dry the back side of forks next to the wheel.

Cleaning the intricate triple-clamp area is easiest to do with a floppy paintbrush. Individual wires are cleaned with a small cloth and stubborn build-up removed with a toothbrush.

For severely chipped front fork pieces, you should consider a full paint job. Remove the front wheel and mask the fender and front of the engine. Use masking tape to protect seals and be sure to mask the fork tubes. Sand as necessary and use spray paint as directed on the label.

Triple-clamp detailing

Triple-clamp areas on dirt bikes consist of the upper and lower clamps, fork tubes, some wiring and cables. On the other side of the spectrum, full-fairing sport bikes hide the triple clamp behind the instrument panel and fairing. The triple clamp is completely enclosed and there is nothing to clean or detail. Full-fairing and instrument panel detailing are covered in Chapter 7.

Cleaning this part on a dirt bike is easy. The space is readily accessible and easily cleaned. Detailing consists of fork tube polishing and possibly some paint work on the clamps. Wires and cables are cleaned, and dressed as desired.

On a Sportster or Enduro-type bike, the triple-clamp area features a headlight and gauges. These items need to be cleaned, and painted parts polished and waxed. The majority of older motorcy-

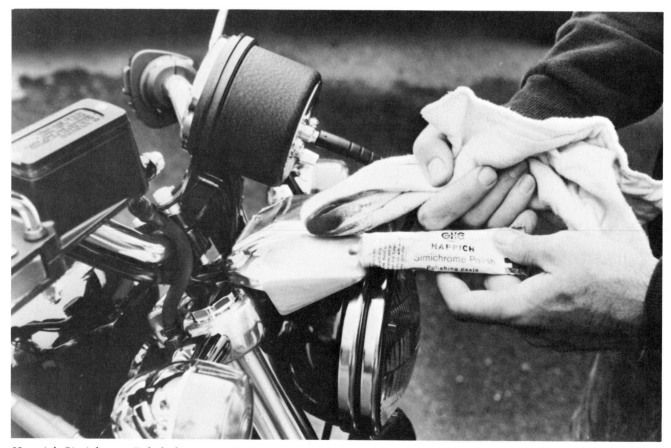

Happich Simichrome Polish does a good job of shining bare metal and chrome pieces. Although the headlight cover on Dan Mycon's Sportster was in good shape, note the amount of dirt and oxidation that came off with just a few polishing strokes.

92

cles feature a different type of design: open triple clamp with headlight assembly, speedometer and tachometer.

Detailed cleaning may require the use of a toothbrush around the area where cables attach to the gauges. Threaded stems and the gnarled ends of cables collect dust and dirt. A paintbrush used around the headlight trim ring during the initial wash should have left this area in good shape. Removing stubborn bug residue deep in the seams between the trim ring, headlight and headlight housing may require the strength of a toothbrush.

Most exposed triple-clamp areas on street-legal motorcycles are busy and intricate with wires, cables, gauges and a headlight. Individual wire cleaning is a good idea, if practical. Most of the time, you will fare well by using a paintbrush dampened with cleaner. Use a soft cloth to wipe away residue. Inserting your index finger inside a cloth sprayed with cleaner is probably the easiest way to clean around gauges and the clamps. Take your time and look for dirt. The more you clean, the more crisp the area will look.

Dressing is applied to wires and cables as needed. Gauge bodies are waxed or dressed, de-pending on the type of material used to coat them. Smooth-painted bodies will need polish and wax, while crinkle-type surfaces may fare better with dressing.

Headlight detailing

Painted headlight housings do come in contact with airborne debris. The results are usually paint chips. Take care of paint problems using the correct paint and the brush from the touch-up paint bottle or an artist's paintbrush. Other than that, polish and wax as you would any painted part.

Stubborn residue on the face of headlights is removed by light scrubbing with an SOS pad or #0000 steel wool and wax. The chrome rings around headlights and alloy covers, like those over Sportster headlights, are shined with chrome polish and then protected with wax. Polish and wax build-up around trim rings and projections on the headlight housings are quickly removed with the cut-off paintbrush.

Extensive detail work calls for the removal of the headlight and cleaning inside the headlight assembly. This will also offer the chance to check electrical wiring connections for corrosion, as well

The swing arm on Squire Tomasie's Flat Tracker receives additional cleaning with a paintbrush. The rub- *ber hose attached to the end of the chain adjuster covers the stem and protects threads from flying grit and gravel.*

as the housing itself. Rubber grommets used to protect wiring inside the assembly are checked for dryness and cracking. All in all, a detailer can inspect every square centimeter of the triple-clamp area. Simply said, everything should be cleaned, waxed or dressed as the surface dictates. Meticulous detailing may even include removing the headlight and cleaning the electrical prongs that protrude from it.

Rear suspension

Rear suspension detailing includes the swing arm and those pieces attached to it, such as the shock absorbers. Dismantle as many items as necessary to gain good access to this area. Motocross bikes do not present much in the way of obstacles, as compared to a Harley Electra Glide. Take off saddlebags, roll bars and chain/belt guards as necessary. Be sure to place these items on a large towel or drop cloth to prevent scratches.

Swing arm cleaning

This part of the motorcycle is subjected to debris kicked up by the rear tire, chain lube spattering and brake dust. A thorough cleaning during the initial wash is a must. Work on one side at a time, and concentrate on build-up still present along ridges, hinge joints and axle bolts.

A brisk wipe with a cleaner-moistened cloth will do well. A toothbrush will make quick work of build-up and a paintbrush will reach trapped debris in shock absorber base brackets. Exhaust pipes on some models will make reaching this area almost impossible. You will have to improvise to clean, or, remove the pipe.

Ideally, the rear wheel and exhaust pipe are removed for complete detailing. Many times, a swing arm will suffer paint chips requiring touch-up. The only way to do this is to dismantle those parts blocking access. Now, if your street bike is only a year or two old with just 3,000 miles on the odometer, this detailed process may not be necessary. On the other hand, if the bike is older and has a lot of miles on it, a complete servicing may be called for.

Swing arm painting

Exceptionally neglected swing arms should be removed, cleaned, sanded and painted. On dirt bikes, this is a relatively easy process since there are few parts attached to the swing arm. Touring bikes present a more complicated process. You

Removing stickers is best done while the bike is new. Residual sticker glue is removed with a dab of solvent or *adhesive remover on a rag. Follow up with cleaner and then wax.*

will have to determine the real need for dismantling and paint work.

Painted swing arms showing oxidation, light scratches or a dull finish are polished and waxed. Complicated, smooth-textured metal swing arms can also be polished and waxed, but the process is painstakingly difficult. You may opt to do this thoroughly once a year when the bike is dismantled. After polishing and waxing, keep the swing arm looking good with frequent (once a week) washing using Simple Green and a floppy paintbrush.

Many swing arms sport stickers and decals. Damaged stickers cannot be repaired and you may consider removing them completely. Check with the motorcycle shop to see if new ones can be purchased. Removing stickers that have been in place for a long time is a process that can result in paint damage.

Some enthusiasts have successfully removed stickers by heating them with a hair blow dryer and then gently and slowly peeling them away. Solvent or paint thinner dabbed on a cloth will wipe away glue leftovers.

Others have had good luck using products designed to loosen sticker glue. Adhesive removers are found at auto parts and auto paint and supply stores. The remover is sprayed on the sticker and its chemical base loosens the glue, allowing you to slowly peel off the sticker without disturbing underlying paint. Removing residual sticker glue is done with a little adhesive remover sprayed on a cloth and wiping.

Shaft drive

Many large motorcycles have been designed with shaft drive instead of chains and sprockets. These present their own unique cleaning and detailing challenges. Drive shafts occasionally leak oil and are susceptible to road grime. They need to be cleaned completely, including the inside surface next to the wheel.

Start with the differential at the wheel and work toward the front of the drive shaft. You will need a small cloth, toothbrush and cleaner. Spray cleaner on the cloth to wipe away smudges and stains. Use the toothbrush to remove build-up from around bolts and ridges. A rag will be fine for absorbing and removing soapy residue.

Road tar and other stubborn pieces of petroleum-based debris may require the use of a solvent or road tar remover. Solvent is relatively safe to use, but check it out on an out-of-the-way

Most of the time, detailed cleaning is done with a paintbrush, toothbrush and cleaner. The assembly on this

BMW is in pretty good shape. Ten or 15 minutes spent detailing will make it look extra crisp.

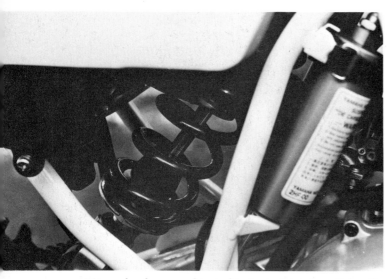

Mono-shocks are subjected to just about everything the rear wheel throws at them. Cleaning may require the use of a plastic brush and paintbrush. Exceptionally dirty shocks should be removed and cleaned separately.

section before applying it to the middle of the shaft housing. Road tar removal products are designed for such use; follow the label instructions carefully to avoid any mishaps.

The majority of shaft cleaning poses no significant problems, except for the side facing the wheel which is hard to reach. Use a toothbrush as best you can. Drape a cleaning cloth over the toothbrush to achieve the final wipedown.

Painted drive shaft housings should be waxed, bare metal ones polished. Application made with your finger inserted in a small cloth affords the best control. Wipe off excess with a clean cloth and use the cut-off paintbrush to remove residue from around bolts and next to ridges.

Shock absorbers

Mono-shocks, hidden in front of the rear tire, present some of the same detailing difficulties as standard spring-equipped shocks attached at the rear of swing arms. The mono-shock body is wiped off with a cloth, connection stems and bolts scrubbed with a toothbrush, and a paintbrush is used on those with outer springs. The degree to which you detail will determine the amount of dismantling required. For those hard-to-reach shocks, you may have to remove the rear wheel. Take unusually dirty shocks off of the bike to clean and touch up paint chips.

Most standard shock absorbers are encased inside a heavy-duty chrome spring. Getting inside the spring to clean the shock body is not always easy. Meticulous cleaning with a paintbrush during the initial wash should leave the body dirt-free. In those instances where shocks remain extra dirty and are riddled with paint chips, take them off and dismantle for complete cleaning and paint touch-up.

Chrome springs are polished with chrome polish and then lightly waxed for protection. For painted bodies, read the label on containers of auto paint polish to determine which one will be right for the paint problem. For example, Meguiar's #4 is designed for heavy oxidation and harsh water spots, while #7 is for removing swirls and spider webbing.

When polishing is complete, apply a light coat of carnauba wax for long-lasting protection of the shine and paint surface. Use the cut-off paintbrush to remove polish and wax build-up in creases and recesses.

Shock absorber dismantling is not difficult. Consult your local motorcycle shop before starting the detail if you have reservations about taking apart the complex shocks on your bike. Take them off one at a time, and be sure to clean and detail the general area around the shock before replacing.

To prevent scratching chrome or painted bolts while replacing shock absorbers, use a ratchet with the right size socket. A heavy-duty plastic freezer bag may be placed over the bolt before applying the socket. Plastic will prevent metal-on-metal contact between the bolt and socket, thus reducing the scratch hazard.

Chapter 7

Fenders, fairing and windshield

Most motorcycles utilize painted fenders and fairings. Care for these items is much the same as the care given to the paint job on your automobile. Gentle washing with a cotton wash mitt and floppy paintbrush should leave the surface clean and scratch-free. Minor oxidation and swirls are removed with polish, while lasting protection is afforded with soft carnauba-based wax.

Fenders on dedicated dirt bikes may be made of flexible plastic. Care for these is not as critical. Ralph Maughn and Wally Shearer have used SOS pads and Comet Cleanser to remove stubborn dirt

Large touring motorcycles feature lots of painted surfaces which require periodic polishing and waxing. The job is made difficult by the amount of obstacles surrounding these surfaces, such as brackets, roll bars, seats and light fixtures.

and scratches from the plastic fenders on their dirt bikes, a cleaning method never advised for painted fenders.

Windshields require special cleaning and polishing products. Light scratches are rubbed out and stubborn bug residue removed using plastic polish, without damaging the clear surface. A light coat of wax, Rain-X or furniture polish helps to shed water while riding in rainy conditions.

Front fender

For the most part, front fenders are readily accessible. Detailed cleaning may be needed on brackets at the forks, mud flaps, attached emblems and add-on lights or reflector accessories. Gentle cleaning with a damp cloth and soft paintbrush should suffice. Cotton swabs work well to clean extra-tight spaces.

Painted fender

Front fenders on most road bikes sit very close to the tire, thus it is not possible to clean the underside without removing the fender or the front wheel. As much as you can, though, try to clean along the bottom edge of the fender to remove any hint of grime build-up.

The type of polish needed to bring back a like-new shine is determined by the condition of fender paint. Sorely neglected paint that is heavily oxidized and scratched needs an application or two of polishing compound. Heavy grit in polishing compound will remove chalky white oxidation and dead paint on the surface. Light scratches, left behind by polishing compound, are buffed out with a

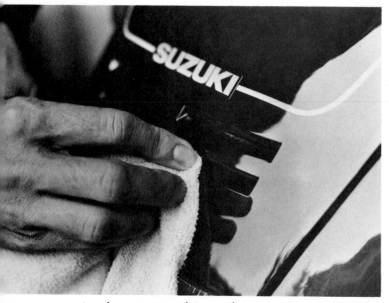

A soft cotton towel is used to remove wax from the louvers on the front fender of Rory Vance's Katana. Controlled wax application helps to eliminate excessive build-up in spaces like this.

milder polish called sealer/glaze, like Meguiar's #7. One application of sealer/glaze may not be enough. Because it is so mild, you may have to apply it two, three or four times in order to achieve a perfect, swirl-free finish.

Art Wentworth prefers to use a small household sponge for polish and wax application. The sponge's firm texture allows him to polish a wide area in one application, and reach into tight spots without the wadding problem of a polishing cloth. The small sponge fits into his hand comfortably and doesn't flop around like the trailing ends of a cloth. All four fingers easily rest on top of the sponge for best manageability and grip.

Thoroughly rinse the applicator sponge in clear water before polishing, to remove old polish or any other potential scratch hazards. Squeeze out excess water until the sponge is just lightly damp. Apply polish to the sponge first and then rub it onto the fender. Wipe in a straight back-and-forth motion to prevent swirls. Use polish sparingly as indicated on the label. Too much polish poured on the sponge will result in excess getting into cracks and seams.

If the fender on your bike is in good condition and presents only a slight dullness, try sealer/glaze first. It is always much better to start polishing with a mild product first and then slowly graduate to a more abrasive polish as needed. Treat paint as you would your skin. It is only so thick, and continuous polishing with a heavy abrasive will wear it down to the primer sooner or later. Shining paint with four applications of sealer/glaze is much milder than one application with polishing compound.

Dry polish is buffed off with a soft dry cloth. Old flannel shirts with the buttons removed work well, as do cotton T-shirts, baby diapers and soft cotton towels. Use the same back-and-forth pattern to remove polish as you did to apply it. Insert the cloth around the fork tube and hold an end in each hand to buff off polish in the tight space around fender brackets, just as you would buff a shoe. Use the cut-off paintbrush as needed along lights and reflectors.

When the fender has been polished to your satisfaction, apply a light coat of protective wax. Dan Mycon prefers to use Mother's on his Sportster, and Squire Tomasie likes Meguiar's for his Kawasaki. Motorcycle enthusiasts are finicky. Once they find a product that works well for them, it is tough to get them to try something new. Basically, any product featuring carnauba wax is good and should offer protection for up to three months, depending on climate, exposure to sunlight and general riding and washing frequency.

Wax application is the same as for polish. Keep the applicator under control and avoid smearing wax over lights and reflectors, emblems, bolts and screw heads. Excess wax in seams and creases makes extra work. Once again, this is where the straight edges on a household sponge come in handy. It is much easier to apply wax around an emblem or reflector with the sponge than it is with a clumsy cloth. Further wax control is achieved by waxing the perimeter of the piece first and then the center.

Plastic fender

Flexible plastic dirt bike fenders are designed to keep mud and rocks from flying into the rider. They are protective devices built to withstand rough riding. Nearly indestructible, they generally will not break or crack even when the bike has been laid down.

Appearance is not nearly as much of a concern with plastic fenders as with painted metal ones. For that reason, detailing is rather plain and simple. Cleaning is accomplished with a wash mitt and soft scrub brush during the initial wash. Further cleaning may call for light scrubbing with a damp SOS pad to remove dirt build-up deep inside scratches.

If the plastic fenders on your dirt bike haven't suffered cuts and scratches from active off-road riding, and still look new and shiny, you may prefer to polish them with an auto paint polish instead of a harsh cleanser or scouring pad. A light coat of wax on the top, as well as the bottom, will help prevent stubborn debris from sticking to the plastic and make future washing easier.

The white plastic fenders on Maughn's dirt bike took a terrific beating during his 2,100 mile Baja trip. Rapid runs through the desert resulted in deep fender scratches from the branches of bushes he clipped along the way. The scratches appeared to intensify as dirt and grime built up in the crevices. Since he traveled on pavement, sand, dirt, gravel and salt water, the fenders were subjected to an exceptionally wide range of debris.

After an initial wash with an SOS pad and Comet Cleanser, Maughn polished the fenders with a sealer/glaze to buff out light scratches and produce a smooth surface. This also helped to remove some dirt still embedded in the hundreds of tiny, yet deep scratches that covered the fender. A final application of Meguiar's #6, a one-step cleaner wax, was used to remove polish stuck in the scratches and to protect the shine.

Chrome fender

Chrome fender cleaning is no different than that for painted fenders. Use a soft wash mitt and a paintbrush to remove dirt from seams and around bolts. Rinse with clear water.

Neglected chrome fenders may be easiest to polish while they are off the bike. This will allow total access to areas concealed by the forks or frame, as well as bracket ends and chrome bolts.

Light polishing is accomplished with a sponge and mild chrome cleaner such as Happich Simichrome. Apply it as you would to any other chrome

piece. As long as some improvement is being made with each polishing, continue until the part meets with your approval.

On the other hand, if the fender is covered with rust deposits and hard to remove build-up, you may have to use #0000 steel wool and polish to bring up the desired shine. Follow this vigorous maneuver with a light application of chrome polish applied with a soft sponge or cloth to remove any minute scratches left behind by the #0000 steel wool.

To keep chrome fenders protected, apply one or two light coats of wax after polishing. Use the cut-off paintbrush to remove polish and wax residue from bolt holes and seams.

Deep scratches on chrome fenders that go through the chrome layer can be touched up with bright silver paint. This will help to hide the scratch until the fender can be rechromed. Depending upon the size of the scratch, use a paper matchstick or artist's paintbrush to apply bright silver paint.

Fairing
Sport bike

Twice a year, Rory Vance removes the lower fairing from his Katana. This allows him to clean the engine and exhaust pipes, and to clean, polish and wax the inside of the fairing.

The biggest hazard in removing the lower fairing on a sport bike is scratches. Put a blanket or tarp

Chrome fenders may be easiest to polish with a small cloth as opposed to a sponge. Reaching brackets and chrome bolts is sometimes difficult. Move obstacles, like cables, out of the way with your free hand. Neglected fenders, brackets and bolts are easiest to polish off the bike.

Before removing the lower fairing from his bike, Vance places a plastic shower curtain on the ground to prevent scratches. The curtain works great for washing the fairing too. Afterward, he hangs it up, rinses it off and lets it air dry.

Bottom fairing sections take a beating. It is quite common for them to be splattered with road tar and other road film. Meguiar's #4 works quite well to clean these pieces and shine dull paint.

on the ground under the fairing before loosening any screws. It is best to have a helper support the free side of the fairing while you loosen the screws on the other side. As you slide the fairing around the engine, be careful not to scratch the fuel tank.

Vance places an old shower curtain on the ground and the fairing on top of it for cleaning. He sprays the inside portion with Simple Green and lets it soak in for a minute or two. Then he washes it with a wash mitt and paintbrush. Accumulations of grease and road oil are sprayed with Gunk and rinsed. Stubborn residue is lightly scrubbed with an SOS pad.

Meguiar's #4 Professional Cleaner is a good polish for removing persistent stains and spots of tar build-up. Vance uses #4 on the inside of the fairing as well as the outer bottom section to polish off encrusted debris and paint blemishes. He follows that with a sealer/glaze and then a coat of carnauba wax.

The outside portion of the fairing is polished and waxed while still on the bike. Twice a year,

Vance polishes the entire bike with a sealer/glaze to remove swirls and old wax, then follows with two very light coats of carnauba wax for protection. Keep in mind that he is a fair-weather rider and keeps his Katana under a cotton cover at all times.

Polishing and waxing the outside portion of the fairing is done just like on any other painted part. Use a soft clean applicator and follow directions on the label. A soft cotton cloth is perfect for removing dried polish and wax. Fold the buffing cloth into quarters, or whatever size suits you, to achieve a manageable towel. As a side becomes soiled, unfold to a clean one. Buffing with a side caked with polish residue can cause swirls.

Use the cut-off paintbrush to remove polish and wax from screw heads, seams, emblems, reflectors and so on. As necessary, employ a toothbrush to remove extra-stubborn residue. Remove resultant dust with a soft cloth.

Touring bike

Fairings on Harley-Davidson Electra Glides and Honda Gold Wings are quite different than those on sport bikes. Touring bike fairings are more intricate, displaying a number of individual lights and bulk as opposed to integration and sleekness. You will do yourself a big favor by spending extra time during the initial wash with a paintbrush and toothbrush, cleaning every nook and cranny on the fairings of these big touring motorcycles before you start in on detailed cleaning.

Detailed cleaning for this type of fairing includes not only removing bug residue from the headlight trim ring, but also the area on the inside

of the fairing next to the footrests and up to the instrument panel.

Removing these types of fairings is impractical, except for the real diehard enthusiast looking for a winter project. Almost all detailing is accomplished with fairings in place.

Take your time to thoroughly inspect inside portions of the lower fairings. Start at the top and work down. Use a clean damp wash mitt and soft dry towel to wipe off light dirt missed during the wash. This includes footrests and roll bars.

The painted parts of the fairing are treated the same as any other painted part: use polishing compound for heavily oxidized paint and severe blemishes, followed by sealer/glaze and then carnauba. Light oxidation and fine swirls do not require the strength of polishing compound. When in doubt, always start with the mildest method first. It is gentler on paint to apply sealer/glaze a number of times than polishing compound once.

A small household sponge applicator works quite well as a polish and wax applicator for these

Fairings feature screw mounts and seams that are prime candidates for polish and wax build-up. Try to avoid direct contact with these parts, choosing instead to wax next to them as opposed to over them.

Detailed cleaning on an open fairing includes washing the inside sections as well as the outside. Paintbrushes offer the best means of reaching into seams and creases to remove dirt and road film.

Oxidized and severely neglected painted fairings are re-juvenated with an application of polishing compound. By far the most abrasive polish, this compound will re-move layers of dead paint to reveal a shiny new surface. Application is made in a straight back-and-forth pattern to avoid swirls.

After using polishing compound, you should polish the surface again using a mild polish such as Eagle 1 Ultra Glaze. This will remove hairline scratches left behind by the compound, and will make paint look new.

New-looking paint will not stay that way unless it is pro-tected with a quality wax. Any carnauba-based wax is good. If the same applicator is to be used for polish and wax, be sure to thoroughly rinse it before applying wax.

types of large fairings. The straight edges work great around lights and trim. Polish chrome accessories with Simichrome or a comparable chrome polish. That application is best made with your finger inserted inside a soft cloth. Buff with a clean soft cloth using the cut-off paintbrush as necessary to remove excess wax from seams and trim.

Encrusted bug residue or road tar on glass light lenses remaining after repeated washing is removed with #0000 steel wool and wax. Dab a wad of steel wool with a liquid glaze or wax and buff. Residue will quickly disappear.

Instrument panel

Electra Glides, Gold Wings, Katanas and ZX-10s feature unique instrument panels. Unlike dirt bikes and some other motorcycles, these machines are designed with a full instrument panel, not just a speedometer and a headlight. Cleaning is not as difficult as one might believe, though.

Once a year, Art Wentworth completely bathes the instrument cluster on his bike with Armor All. The polypenetrant is worked in with a paintbrush so that every square inch of the panel is

Once a year, at the most, Art Wentworth likes to completely bathe vinyl instrument panels in Armor All. He figures the in-depth coverage will last a long time and protect vinyl from the sun's ultraviolet rays. After the dressing has had time to soak in, he washes the bike completely to remove excessive dressing from non-vinyl as well as vinyl pieces.

Dressing is worked into vinyl and tight spots along seams and switches with a clean paintbrush to ensure complete coverage.

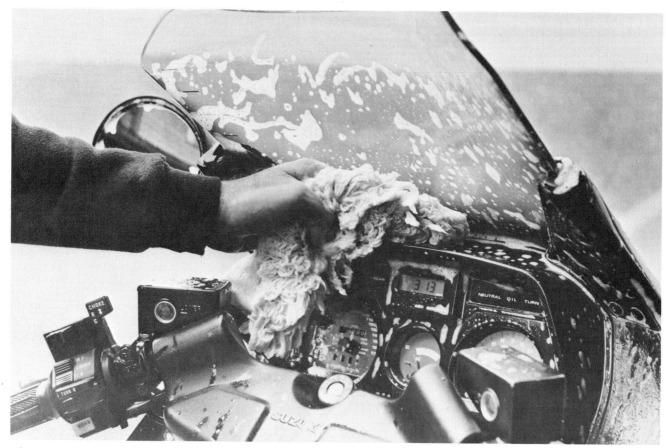

Thorough washing of the instrument panel is accomplished with a wash mitt and plenty of soapsuds. This *removes excess dressing from the surface of vinyl and leaves it looking rich, not glossy.*

This is what the instrument panel on Rory Vance's Katana looked like after Art Wentworth bathed it in Armor All and washed it. The vinyl is crisp looking and presents a uniform degree of light gloss, like it did when new.

touched. Then, he washes the motorcycle completely, including the instrument panel. Washing removes excess dressing and leaves the surface looking new.

Not everyone agrees with Wentworth's method. Many prefer to keep the instrument panel clean and out of the sun. By the way, sunlight is an instrument panel's worst enemy. The ultraviolet rays will dry out gauge faces, as well as surrounding vinyl in very short time. If you must park your motorcycle outdoors on a daily basis, buy a motorcycle cover. If that is not within your means, park the bike in such a way that the sun will not beat down on gauges for extended periods of time.

About the only way to completely clean all of the seams and grooves on an intricate instrument panel and handlebar controls is with a paintbrush and toothbrush. Items missed during the initial wash are picked up with a damp brush and dry towel. CB and intercom radio controls sport lots of buttons and knobs. The thin bristles of a paintbrush reach inside grooves to dislodge pieces of grit, dust and dirt build-up. During dry months, use the brush attachment on a vacuum cleaner to quickly remove accumulations of dust and lint.

This method of cleaning is especially good for radio speakers.

Windshield

Motorcycle windshields are constantly bombarded by road hazards and bugs. If cleaned immediately, these problems easily wash away. However, on an extended road trip, they may be allowed to dry, making removal more difficult.

As with painted parts, always start with the mildest method first and work up to the more abrasive. Lots of soap and water during the initial wash should loosen or dissolve even the most stubborn bug residue. On those occasions where soap and water do not remove the problem, try plastic polish. It is less abrasive than plastic cleaner.

If repeated attempts with plastic polish fail to remove the blemish, use plastic cleaner. There are times when you will have to apply cleaner and then use your fingernail to lightly scratch the blemish off. You stand a slight chance of creating minute scratches with the cleaner, but polish will remove hairline scratches left behind, and the end result will be a crystal-clear windshield.

Overall windshield cleaning must be thorough. To be ensured of a swirl-free windshield, always wipe plastic cleaner and polish in a straight up-and-down pattern; refrain from applying them in a circular motion. A clean damp sponge makes a good applicator, and a soft cotton towel is best for a buffer.

Some motorcycles are equipped with retractable windshields, like Rory Vance's Katana. When detailing the windshield on these models, make sure the windshield is in its full upright position. Don't forget to clean the inside of the windshield as well.

Rear fender

Accessibility to rear fenders is not always easy. On most road bikes, only the tail of the fender is visible. Detailed cleaning is accomplished only when saddlebags are removed and the seat opened or taken off.

The soft bristles of a damp paintbrush will remove light accumulations of dirt in tight spaces next to saddlebag brackets, frame and the taillight assembly. Use a soft cloth to wipe away residue and moisture streaks. As necessary, dab a cotton swab into bolt hole recesses and Allen heads to remove dirt build-up.

Polish and wax application is tricky because of obstructions such as wires, support brackets, taillights and license plates. Removing the license plate allows access to a wide part of the fender. Dismantling is easy, generally requiring the removal of only two screws. Use your free hand to hold wires out of the way, and take your time polishing and waxing around brackets and other obstruc-

Plastic Polish is a mild abrasive designed to clean and shine windshields and other plastic items. Follow the directions on the label for best results.

tions. If the sponge is too big for use in certain tight spots, try inserting your finger inside a clean damp cloth for controlled application.

Polish and wax removal is done with a clean soft cloth. In this area, the cut-off paintbrush works well to remove polish and wax residue from the base of the taillight, flush-mounted reflectors and screw heads.

Polishing and waxing next to seats and other vinyl and rubber parts is most easily controlled by using an applicator with a straight edge. Apply a small amount of wax on the sponge to help prevent smears on these parts.

Taillight assembly

Motorcycle taillight assemblies range from the simple light and license plate bracket on Mycon's Sportster to the exotic integrated stop light and turn signal model featured on Tomasie's ZX-10. On either assembly, cleaning is done with a toothbrush, paintbrush and soft cloth.

The most frequently overlooked detail item on taillights is wax residue around lettering on the plastic lens. Use a toothbrush to quickly remove this build-up. Minor scratches on plastic lenses are polished out with Meguiar's #17 Professional Plastic Cleaner, followed by Meguiar's #10 Professional Plastic Polish. The polish is designed to be used by itself, after the cleaner. If scratches are very fine, you may have the best luck using polish only, applying it more than once to mildly restore the lens' clarity. Be sure to read and follow the instructions on the label.

Once in a while, lens screws loosen and allow moisture to enter the light assembly, causing the lens to fog up. Remove the lens and dry with a soft cloth. Clean the rest of the assembly with a paint-brush and cloth. Moisture is absorbed from tight spots with a paper towel. Check the rubber seal to be sure it is in good condition before replacing the lens.

After 2,100 miles in Baja, the inside portion of Ralph Maughn's Yamaha taillight became quite dusty. The reason was a cracked lens. After removing the lens and cleaning the entire assembly, he glued the lens back together with clear silicone. It has held ever since. Maughn has had good luck using silicone to glue various plastic pieces back together, with no failures to date.

License plate

Dan Mycon and Art Wentworth believe license plates and license plate frames are a focal point at the rear of any motorcycle. Both have taken pains to make sure their plate assemblies match the overall appearance of the motorcycle.

Primarily, a gaudy dealer plate frame may prove beneficial as an advertising aid, but does that frame make your motorcycle look better? If the

Moisture in tight spaces inside taillights is wicked up with a paper towel. The thin nature of paper towels allows easy access under bulb assemblies.

A paintbrush is used to clean a taillight lens. Use a toothbrush to remove dirt and debris from the outer edge to ensure a clean surface and good seal next to the taillight gasket.

back of your bike sports lots of chrome, consider using a simple chrome frame with chrome screws. If black is the most prevalent color, install a simple black frame with black screws.

Even though the two holes at the bottom of the license plate do not lead to a part of the bracket, fill them with screws to add balance to the entire plate. Wentworth likes to line up all the screw heads in a vertical position. He says it helps them to drain water and prevent rust. In reality, he is just meticulous and likes everything in order.

License tabs should be attached in line with the symmetry of the license plate. Cockeyed tabs throw off the balance of the motorcycle, causing it to appear awkward. Attention to this kind of detail is what allows one bike to stand tall and look crisp in comparison to another.

License tabs are best applied in warm temperatures. If you have to attach new ones in cold weather, take the plate off of the bike and bring it into the house to warm up. Be sure it is clean and free of road film. If you have purchased a used bike and the tabs are crooked, you can try loosening the tab glue with a blow dryer. After it is warm, gently peel off the tab and replace it in the correct position.

This is the Arlen Ness Billet custom license plate frame on Dan Mycon's Sportster. It looks crisp, tidy, uniform and blends well with the motorcycle.

Chapter 8

Fuel tank

Many motorcycle enthusiasts see the fuel tank on their bike as a focal point for the entire machine. This is why many owners have customized their tanks with pinstripes and special paint work. Detailing fuel tanks is not an intricate chore. Consci-

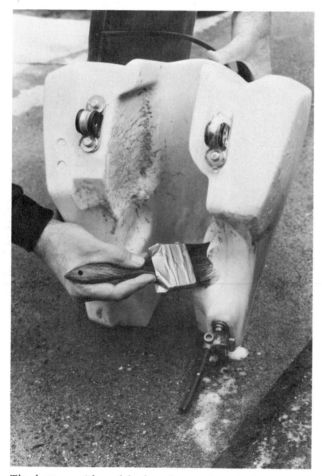

The bottom sides of fuel tanks are frequently covered with layers of dust. During an annual detail, turn them upside down to clean, polish and wax the underside. Be extremely cautious while doing this to avoid spilling gasoline.

entious cleaning, polishing and waxing will help almost any tank look new.

General cleaning

During the course of a complete detail, the fuel tank will have to be removed to allow access to the frame and top of the engine. It is best to have the least amount of fuel possible in the tank at the time of its removal. The tank will weigh less with a minimal amount of fuel in it, making it easier to handle.

Place the tank on a large towel or piece of cardboard so it doesn't get scratched. The dirtiest parts will be the bottom and fuel valve. You will need a cleaning cloth, toothbrush and cleaner for effective cleaning.

Use a clean, damp wash mitt to wipe off the bottom of the tank. Most of the cleaning consists of dust removal, although you may come across some build-up requiring the strength of a cleaner. Spray cleaner on a cleaning cloth and then apply. If necessary, spray cleaner directly on dirt build-up to help loosen and dissolve it. Wipe off residue and overspray with a clean cloth.

The edges along frame mount brackets on the inner part of the tank may need to be scrubbed with a toothbrush to dislodge dirt build-up. Spray the bristles with cleaner and wipe off residue with a cloth. Seams at the bottom of the tank are another place where build-up accumulates. A fold in the cleaning cloth may be all that is needed to clean next to ridges and seams. If not, use a soft toothbrush.

Fuel valves always seem to collect dust and dirt. Washing these valves with a paintbrush during the initial wash makes detailed cleaning easier. Their design requires the use of a toothbrush for definitive cleaning around the petcock, screw heads and body. Be sure to clean the base of the valve where it attaches to the tank. This edge is frequently caked with a layer of dust and dirt.

Use caution when tipping the tank over to reach the fuel valve. Most fuel caps tighten securely but may leak in an upside-down position.

Fuel valves collect an abundance of dirt and grime, especially on dirt bikes. Use a toothbrush to remove accumulations along ridges and screws.

To remove rust and scale build-up from the inside of a neglected tank, Steve Giblin uses Naval Jelly and a handful of small nuts and bolts. As the tank is shook up and down and side to side, the nuts and bolts scrape off rust and scale and allow better penetration for the Naval Jelly.

After the tank has been cleaned, thoroughly rinsed with clear water and completely dried, Giblin uses Fuel Tank Sealant to coat the inner surface of the tank. This helps to seal against small leaks and prevent future rust build-up.

Gasoline is an extremely flammable liquid. Its vapors are heavier than air and will hang low, close to the ground. These vapors can be ignited by the pilot light on natural gas hot water heaters or any other heat source. If a spill should occur, quickly wipe it up with a rag and rinse the spill area with water.

Inside the tank

It is not uncommon for varnish-type films to accumulate on the inside of fuel tanks. Gasoline additives are sold at motorcycle shops to help thwart these formations, and enthusiasts have used them with varied success. Neglected tanks that have sat empty for extra-long periods may be prone to rust and will have to be thoroughly cleaned and sealed before being put to use.

Cleaning

Steve Giblin has had good results removing varnish-type films from the inside of fuel tanks using solvent. With the tank empty and off of the motorcycle, he pours a quart, or so, of solvent into it, replaces the cap and then vigorously shakes it. The agitation of the solvent against the bottom, sides and top of the tank loosens varnish and leaves the surface clean. This maneuver is done twice and sometimes more often, depending upon the amount of varnish.

Extra-tough film residue may require more than just solvent to remove. In those cases, Giblin has placed a handful of small nuts and bolts inside the tank along with the solvent. The scraping of the nuts and bolts against the tank's inner body break loose varnish and allow solvent to further wash away residue. When the results are satisfactory, he

A straight back-and-forth pattern is best for applying polish and wax. For that matter, anytime you rub on a surface, it should be done in this pattern to avoid the creation of swirls.

will rinse the tank one more time with clean solvent to wash away any lingering residue. Solvent is emptied through the cap. Then, he removes the petcock, or fuel valve, to allow the tank to dry completely.

Rust removal

Removing rust from the inside of fuel tanks will require a stronger solution than solvent. Giblin has used Naval Jelly and Metal Prep successfully. Both are potent products and you must read the directions on the label to prevent unwanted damage to the tank. (You should also wear heavy-duty rubber gloves and eye protection.)

Once again, Giblin places a handful of small nuts and bolts inside the tank before pouring in the Naval Jelly or Metal Prep. The tank is vigorously shaken and then allowed to sit for the prescribed amount of time, generally about five minutes. He has allowed tanks to sit for up to a half an hour, but they were in terrible condition and this was a last resort.

After the allotted time has elapsed, the tank is thoroughly rinsed with plenty of water. (Once again, you must use caution and should wear heavy-duty rubber gloves to prevent residue from landing on your skin.) Once the tank has been adequately rinsed, with no residue remaining, he allows it to dry. Giblin speeds this process by rinsing the tank with alcohol or lacquer thinner. These products quickly help to dissipate water but are also very flammable. (You must be extra cautious with their use. Do this outside and far away from any open flame, such as a water heater pilot light.)

Tank coatings

Once a fuel tank has been vigorously cleaned, especially with harsh chemicals, it should be coated with a tank sealant. These products are not easy to find and you should shop around for them before you start the project.

Giblin uses a product called Fuel Tank Sealant made by Lubri Tech. Other products are available and may be found at motorcycle shops, auto parts stores and auto body paint and supply stores. Chances are, motorcycle mechanics are most familiar with these sealants and they should be able to direct you to a source of supply.

Fuel Tank Sealant is made for motorcycle tanks. Lubri Tech recommends one pint per three gallon tank capacities. The label also states that it is good for metal, ABS plastic and fiberglass tanks. Twenty-four hours is the recommended drying time.

Sealant is poured into the tank and then swished around so all surfaces are covered. The label advises to set the tank on the front end for drying. Some mechanics have had better luck removing the petcock and allowing excess sealant to drain through that hole. They claim that setting the tank on its front end allowed excess sealant to build up at the front of the inside of the tank, causing an extra thick layer to form. They prefer an even layer distribution and therefore choose to allow excess to drain out the petcock hole and back into the can of sealant placed at the hole.

These tips are good and have worked for some motorcycle mechanics. However, if you have no experience working with fuel tank sealers, you must read the directions on the label of the product you use and follow them to the letter. Inappropriate use of sealant products may leave spots inside the tank uncoated. These spots could deteriorate and may cause flakes of rust to enter the fuel system and plug carburetor jets which will cause the bike to stop running.

Rust prevention

The best way to prevent rust from forming inside the tank is to use it. Keep it filled most all the time and drive the bike on a frequent basis. Most rust problems occur when the tank is only partially filled with fuel and the motorcycle is stored for a long period. Moisture is attracted to the inside of the tank and sits on the inner walls creating rust formations.

If your bike is to be stored for a long period, consider using a gasoline additive designed to prevent condensation. Also, make sure the cap fits securely and the gasket inside the cap is in good shape.

Painted tanks
Polishing

Oxidized fuel tanks have to be polished. Meguiar's has an excellent selection of sealers and glazes. Read the labels on each product until you find one designed for the type of polishing problem your tank presents. It is best to start with a mild polish, saving more abrasive compounds for severe problems.

If you have to use polishing compound for heavy oxidation and scratch removal, apply mild polish afterward to buff off swirls and spider webbing. Take your time and avoid smearing polish on accessory parts like rubber pads and emblems. If possible, remove obstructions such as fuel caps, seats and raised metal emblems.

Tanks that have been removed should be polished and waxed off of the bike for ease of application and complete coverage. Polish and wax the underside of the tank, as well as the inner portion that fits over the frame.

Polishing tanks on sport bikes is made difficult because of obstructions. Embedded rubber and vinyl pads, screws, fairing seams and fuel tank caps are susceptible to polish build-up. A small rectangular sponge applicator is easily maneuvered around these obstructions and will help to reduce build-up.

When polish has dried, use a soft, clean cotton cloth to buff. Move the cloth in a straight back-and-forth motion to avoid swirls or spider webbing. The cut-off paintbrush makes quick work of removing residue from seams, grooves and screw heads.

Apply polish as many times as necessary to achieve a perfect paint finish. As long as a mild polish shows improvement after each application, continue to use it until the finish is right. It is better to use a mild polish a number of times as opposed to an abrasive polish once.

Newer motorcycle fuel tanks may have been painted with a clear coat. This is simply a few coats of clear lacquer over the color coat. The dealer should advise you of this at the time of purchase. Another way to tell is by looking at stick-on decals. With no clear coat over them, decal edges are crisp and you can feel the rigid definition of the edge. Those covered with clear coat are smooth; decal edges are more or less rounded off.

Clear-coat paint finishes are shined and waxed with products designed for clear coats. Meguiar's #2 Professional Hi-Tech Cleaner is specially blended for removing oxidation and scratches from clear-coat paints. Meguiar's #9 Professional Hi-Tech Swirl Remover is a milder polish used to remove very fine scratches on clear coats. Other manufacturers also make polish products for clear coats. You will have to read their labels to see which one meets your needs.

Waxing

Waxing the tank entails the same technique as polishing. Use a straight back-and-forth pattern. Two light coats are better than one heavy one. Avoid smearing wax on seats, rubber pads and

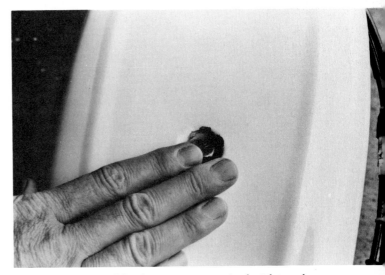

Minor paint chips, like this one, are repaired with touch-up paint. Use the brush attached to the cap of touch-up paint, or use a fine artist's paintbrush.

screw heads. Wax goes on and comes off best in warm temperatures. If you are detailing during a cold month, wax inside a garage to maintain some warmth on the surface.

The brand of wax used is up to you. Dan Mycon likes Mother's, Squire Tomasie likes Meguiar's, and others have had luck with Turtle Wax, Simoniz and Eagle 1. The basic ingredient in any good wax is carnauba, so as long as the product you use has carnauba, you will get good results.

Paste and cream waxes seem to last the longest. Liquids are thinned down, and sprays have to be thinned down even more in order to spray through tiny nozzles. Just how long a wax job lasts depends on the conditions it is subjected to. If the motorcycle is parked in a garage most of the time and ridden only on fair-weather days, a wax job could last six months or more. On the other hand, a wax job on a bike ridden daily and always parked in the sun will last only about four to six weeks.

Paint touch-up

Touch-up paint for motorcycle tanks is available at motorcycle shops. If a special color is needed, you will have to go to an auto body paint and supply store. This facility can match perfectly just about any kind of automotive or motorcycle paint.

Touch-up paint comes in a small bottle. A brush is attached to the inside of the cap and is used to apply paint to slight nicks, chips and

Pinstripes are a common means for customizing paint jobs. Professional pinstripers are actually artists; they design and apply stripes with a steady hand. You can achieve the same basic results with pinstripe tape, like this stripe on Dan Mycon's Sportster.

scratches. Other than that, use an artist's paintbrush.

If touch-up paint work is anticipated, do not apply any polish or wax to the area until paint work is done. Polish and wax prevent paint from coming in contact with the base material, and the touch-up will turn out looking terrible.

Clean the nick, chip or scratch thoroughly. If you believe wax, polish or another substance is still on the chip, wipe the spot with a cloth dabbed in Prepsol or other solvent. The surface must be completely clean and free of dirt, grease, polish and wax.

Significant paint chips are masked off. An easy way to do this is to punch a hole in a piece of masking tape with a paper hole punch. Place the tape on the tank, with the chip exposed through the hole. Lightly apply a coat of touch-up and let it dry according to instructions on the label. Then, apply additional coats in the same manner until the layer of paint on the chip is slightly higher than surrounding paint.

When, according to the label, paint has cured long enough to withstand sanding (generally a week), mask the chip the same way you did when painting. Masking tape protects those areas around the chip during sanding. Use #600 wet-and-dry sandpaper to smooth the chip to about the same height as surrounding paint. Remove the masking tape and use polishing compound to further smooth the painted chip to blend with the rest of the paint. Follow with a couple of applications of sealer/glaze and then carnauba.

Pinstripes

Pinstripe painting is an art. It takes a steady hand and a vivid imagination to come up with some of the unique designs featured on customized motorcycles. The easiest way to apply pinstripes to the fuel tank on your motorcycle is to hire a professional to do the job. It is also the most expensive way, however.

Pinstripe tape is an acceptable alternative to actual painted pinstripes. This tape is available at most auto parts and auto body paint and supply stores. Motorcycle shops don't generally carry pinstripe tape, although they may have access to specialty decals for specific makes and models.

Application of pinstripe tape is easy. It is not immediately permanent and can easily be lifted off of the surface after it is put on for adjustment. Have a good idea of what the design will be before you start, though. Putting it on and taking it off more than once will reduce the adhesive power of the glue, and the tape may not stick as well as you'd prefer. After the package is opened, pinstripe tape has a shelf life of about six months. To keep leftover tape in good condition for a longer period, enclose it in a Zip-Lock plastic bag or any other plastic bag that can be sealed.

To start out, peel back a few inches of backing paper. Apply the open section where you want it, and hold the remaining section in line with where you intend it to be placed.

Rather than hold the entire roll of pinstripe tape during application, cut off a section that is just a little longer than needed. The trailing edge can hang down while installing the other end. Pull off a few inches of backing paper and apply tape. Then, continue to pull off just a few inches of backing paper at a time, and install the tape little by little. Around corners and curves, use your free hand to hold tape in place while stretching the rest of the tape and securing it in place.

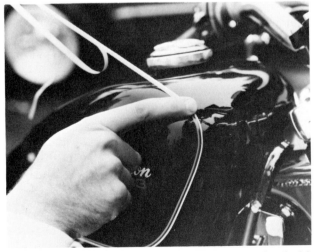

While going around corners, use your free hand to hold the corner in place. Gradually slide your free hand along the tape to secure it in place as your other hand guides it into position.

Cutting pinstripes is critical. Too much pressure applied to the razor blade will cause it to cut the paint on your tank. Use a very light touch, choosing to go over the cut two or three times to effect the incision.

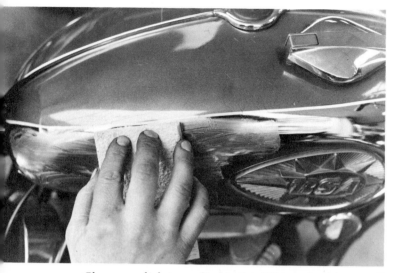

Chrome polish is applied to this BSA tank with a small sponge. The straight edge of the sponge allows good control along the painted edge to prevent rubbing off paint.

Cutting the tape is the most critical part of the job. Use a sharp new razor blade. Hold the blade steady by resting your hand on the tank. Very lightly, cut the tape at the angle you want. Do not use so much force that the blade digs into the paint under the tape, however. The ends can be cut at angles, points or whatever you want.

Parallel pinstripe tape is also available. This kind of tape features two pinstripes about an eighth

A folded piece of soft cotton flannel is used to wipe off dried chrome polish from the chrome tank on this 1970 BSA A65. Polish residue is removed from the edge of the BSA emblem with a cut-off paintbrush.

of an inch apart. They are held together with backing paper and a clear plastic film over the top. Do *not* pull the clear plastic film off of the tape until the tape is in its final, permanent position. If the film was removed and you wanted to move the tape, you would have a difficult time perfectly matching the two pieces. The clear film holds them in place parallel to each other, making the overall job easier.

Chrome tanks

Chrome fuel tanks are commonly found on custom motorcycles and older English bikes. It is easiest and most effective to detail the tank off of the motorcycle. General cleaning is done much the same as painted tanks. Stubborn stains are removed with mild polish, like Simichrome.

Polishing

There is no need to use a harsh polish to shine a tank that is already in good shape. To remove a fine film of dirt and brighten a slightly dull chrome tank, use mild auto polish like Meguiar's #7. If the results are less than satisfactory, graduate to chrome polish and apply with a damp sponge.

Neglected chrome fuel tanks spotted with rust and fuel stains will require more vigorous polishing. Use caution next to painted parts on the tank. Aggressive polishing could wear down and remove paint. This is where the straight edge of a small sponge is handy and easily guided along paint lines.

Polish can also be applied with a soft cloth. Insert two fingers into the cloth and dab on a bit of polish. Then, work a small section at a time making the application in a straight back and forth direction, just like polishing paint. After each application, wipe off polish residue with a clean soft towel. Continue polishing and wiping until the tank shines to your expectations.

Polish residue can be dislodged from tank emblems and insignias with the cut-off paintbrush. However, most of these tank emblems are attached by only two screws and it is much easier to remove them before polishing.

Waxing

Chrome tanks should also be treated to one or two light coats of carnauba wax after polishing. This will help to protect the tank from future fuel spills and other debris. Application of wax is made the same as with painted tanks. Keep your hands covered with a clean towel while handling the tank to prevent the formation of fingerprints on the finely polished and waxed chrome. The same towel can be used to handle the tank while replacing it back on the bike to prevent smudges during installation.

Plastic tanks

Large-capacity plastic fuel tanks are common on desert and motocross bikes. If a good coat of wax is not maintained on this type of tank from the start, it will be subject to permanent stains from gasoline and other petroleum-based products.

The white plastic desert tank on Ralph Maughn's Yamaha was streaked with fuel stains after the Baja trip. He used SOS pads and Comet Cleanser to clean the tank, but they did not completely remove the stains. A number of polishing products were also tried, including polishing compound. Nothing worked and the faint stains are still on the tank.

Sunlight, age and normal wear and tear seem to break down the surface of plastic tanks. A brand-new tank will not stain as easily as the one on Maughn's Yamaha. Over time, it appears as though pores open up on plastic tanks, which allows fuel to penetrate the surface and become bonded to it, causing stains.

The best way to prevent this from happening is to maintain a frequent cleaning and waxing schedule. Wash the bike after every ride, polish and wax the tank anytime fuel has been spilled on it.

Gas caps

Most fuel tank caps are simple and require little work to get them looking good. Take caps off of the bike and use a soft cloth and cleaner to remove dust and dirt. Use a toothbrush along the outer ring to dislodge dirt trapped inside the grip grooves. Chrome caps are shined with chrome polish and painted caps polished with sealer/glaze. A light coat of wax on both types is a good idea.

You should check the bottom side of caps for dirt and gasket condition. Remove dirt as necessary. New gaskets can be purchased at the motorcycle shop.

Harley-Davidson sells an aftermarket gas cap with an intricate metal badge attached to the top. Cleaning this kind of ornate item is done off of the bike, and will require a toothbrush and cotton swabs. Dan Mycon has such a gas cap on his Sportster. He sprays cleaner on the toothbrush and then scrubs the badge. A cotton swab is used to reach into recesses to remove dirt.

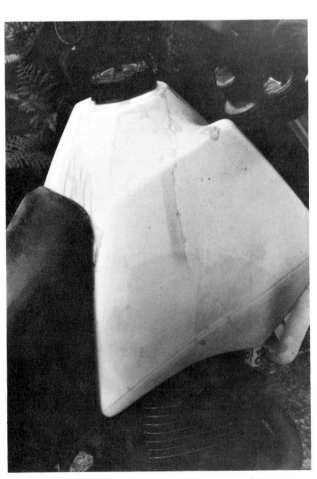

Plastic desert tanks are susceptible to gasoline stains. Removing stains is not always possible, as they tend to impregnate plastic. From the start, attempt to avoid this problem by maintaining a good coat of wax on the tank.

Comet Cleanser and steel wool soap pads were used to try and remove gasoline stains from the tank on Ralph Maughn's bike. A good deal of residue was removed, but slight discoloration persisted. The complete tank was scrubbed, rinsed with clear water and then scrubbed again. It took three to four scrubbings to fade deeply embedded stains.

After the ultra-vigorous scrub, Maughn's tank was polished with Meguiar's #6. This is a one-step cleaner wax that includes petroleum distillates. It works quite well to clean, shine and protect, although it does not last as long as carnauba wax.

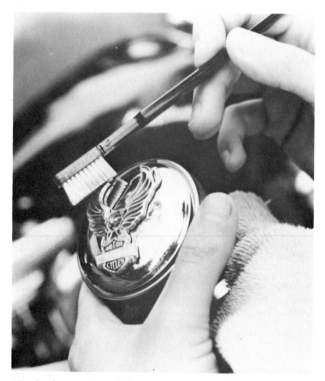

The badge on top of the ornate gas cap of Dan Mycon's Sportster features deep valleys which can be cleaned only with a toothbrush. Cotton swabs are also used to absorb and remove lingering water and dirt residue from the valleys on this gas cap badge. Then Dan Mycon uses his wife's blow dryer to dry his Sportster's ornate gas cap completely. This maneuver works quite well to evaporate tiny pockets of water in tough-to-reach spots.

After rinsing with water, Mycon shakes the cap to throw off water. He uses dry cotton swabs to absorb moisture caught inside the design, and has even used his wife's blow dryer to speed the drying process.

The fuel cap on Rory Vance's Katana is built into the tank; it cannot be removed for cleaning. This type can be polished, but one must be careful to avoid smearing polish on the painted tank. To maintain the best control, stick your finger into a cloth and hold the rest of the cloth in the palm of your hand to keep it out of the way. Dab your finger with polish and slowly shine as necessary.

The holes on Allen head screws that secure the fuel cap to Vance's fuel tank were starting to rust. He twisted cotton swabs sprayed with cleaner into the holes to remove debris. Stubborn spots required the swab to be dipped in paint thinner for complete cleaning. Dry swabs were used to absorb moisture and remove remaining residue.

When the screws were completely clean and dry, Vance used the end of a paper matchstick to apply bright silver Rust-oleum paint to the center of the screws. The paint was almost a perfect match to the silver screws. When completed, the screws looked new and the fuel cap assembly was crisp.

Tank protection

Squire Tomasie likes to ride his ZX-10 fast. As a racer, he knows how to handle motorcycles at

The gas cap on Rory Vance's Katana is built-in. Allen head screws attach it to the tank. Cotton swabs were used to clean the center holes on rusty Allen head screws. First sprayed with cleaner, the swabs were twisted into each hole to break loose and absorb dirt and rust residue. Further cleaning included just a dab of paint thinner on the end of cotton swabs. You can see how much residue was extricated from the screw head.

high speeds. Much of the time, his knees are firmly pressed against the fuel tank. This gives him stability and helps gain more control.

After a few hundred miles, scratches and wear spots were starting to develop on the tank of Tomasie's bike. They were a result of his knees rubbing against it. Light polishing and wax removed the dullness. But in no time at all, smears and scratches reappeared. Unless something was done, these two spots on the tank were going to rub through to the metal.

Art Wentworth came up with an idea of placing clear plastic film over those areas to protect them against scratching. Plastic would absorb the abuse, and the clear texture would allow the tank's true color to show through.

Tomasie made a template out of a piece of paper that conformed to the shape of the tank. After the template was cut out, he laid it over a piece of clear number plate plastic and marked it. With the plastic cut to shape, the backing was peeled off one edge and the plastic was attached in place. The remaining backing paper was peeled off a few inches

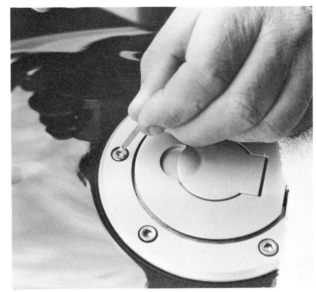

Carefully, Rory Vance used the clean end of a paper matchstick to apply bright silver Rust-oleum paint to the screws. A fine artist's paintbrush could have been used instead of the matchstick. The results were excellent.

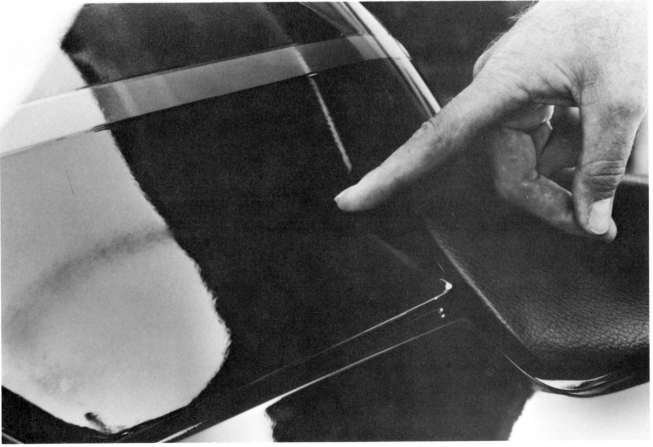

A rounded, dull smear is noticeable at the left bottom part of the picture. This is where Squire Tomasie's knee has been wearing a spot on the tank of his ZX-10. Polish *and wax remove the smear handily, but continued chafing will ruin the paint.*

A template was made out of paper to conform with the shape of the fuel tank. Careful attention was given to stripes and contours featured on the tank. Using the template, a tracing was made on the clear plastic num- ber plate. The template was matched to the other side of the tank, but had to be turned over when it came time to trace it for the other side's plastic.

at a time, and the plastic was attached and smoothed. The results were clean and crisp, and blended well with the rest of the bike.

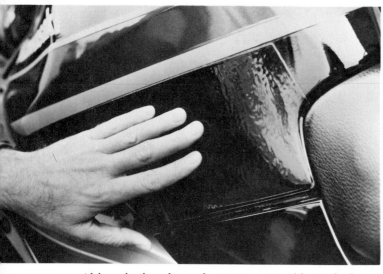

Although the clear plastic is noticeable, it looks as though it is part of the bike. This addition will prolong the life of the paint underneath, and Squire Tomasie doesn't have to worry about scratching the tank when he hugs it with his knees while riding fast.

Chapter 9

Seat, saddlebags and extras

Motorcycles appear quite simple when compared to other types of motorized vehicles. Basically, all that one initially sees is an engine, two wheels, a fuel tank, handlebars and seat. Once a detailer starts to clean and polish, however, he or she soon recognizes there is a lot more to a motorcycle than meets the eye. The surface area is enormous and there are a lot of extra parts and projections to detail.

Along with the painted frame, fairing and fuel tank, there are numerous chrome, rubber and vinyl accessories. Each piece may require special attention, and what is good for one may not be good for another. For instance, dressing may help to rejuvenate a weathered vinyl instrument housing, but could make a dull vinyl seat too slippery, turning it into a potential riding hazard.

Detailing extras include special attention to specific problems and unique motorcycle attrib-utes. Although your bike should be exceptionally clean and tidy by this point, concentration on particular pieces add bonus points to the overall detail and make your motorcycle stand tall and look crisp and stunning.

New bike preparation

A brand-new motorcycle fresh off the showroom floor may need some detailing. It is a good idea to wash and wax it as soon as possible, to ensure that an adequate amount of wax is on painted surfaces to protect them against road hazards and debris.

New bikes from overseas will most likely be covered with Cosmolene. This is a product that

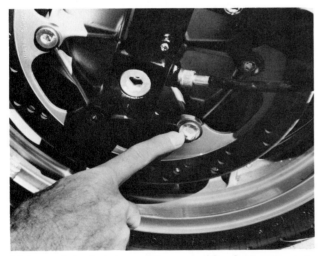

Motorcycle technicians at the assembly plant put paint-type marks on nuts and bolts to designate that they have been torqued to specifications, and to signify that the part assembly is complete. These marks are removed with solvent and a toothbrush and then washed with soap and water.

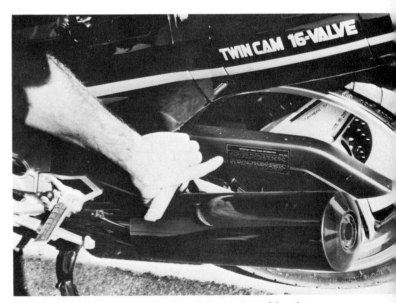

New bikes feature a variety of service stickers like this one on the chain guard of Squire Tomasie's new ZX-10. Many enthusiasts prefer to remove these stickers. Take them off when the motorcycle is new and while adhesive is fresh and has yet to penetrate paint. Most stickers peel off easily. Use a fingernail to gently loosen a corner and then slowly and evenly pull it away from the surface.

Since service stickers include various specifications dealing with drive chains and load data, you might consider saving the stickers by taping them to a clean piece of paper. The paper is then folded and kept with other papers relating to the bike.

Heavy-textured motorcycle seats easily withstand vigorous scrubbing with a plastic-bristled brush. This method is required for heavily soiled seats, like this one on Ralph Maughn's dirt bike.

protects metal from the severe corrosion problems associated with salt water exposure. Peter Danikas has had good luck using Gunk to remove Cosmolene.

A number of service and information stickers may be attached to your new motorcycle. It is common to find them on chain guards, swing arms, fenders and frame. Some enthusiasts prefer to leave them on in the belief that they add originality to their bike. Others, such as Squire Tomasie, usually take them off. If you have chosen to remove these stickers, do it soon, before sunlight has a chance to bake them on.

For the most part, stickers on new bikes come off easily. The most secure way to remove stickers and prevent paint damage is to use an adhesive remover. These products are sold at auto parts and auto paint and supply stores. Spray them directly on stickers to loosen glue. Cleanup and glue residue is wiped off with a towel dabbed in remover. Further cleaning is done with sealer/glaze, and you should finish the job with a coat of carnauba-based wax.

Always read the owners manual before attempting any service work. You may be required to use certain lubricating products at specific intervals in order to keep the warranty in effect. Follow the manufacturer's recommendations for break-in operation before you start riding at high speeds. After the first ride, check nuts, bolts and screws for tightness. You should also inspect the chain, hand levers, foot levers and fluid reservoirs to ensure they are in proper order.

Vinyl seats

Seats are easiest to clean off of the bike. Heavy-textured vinyl seats may need to be scrubbed with a plastic brush and cleaner. Use a toothbrush along beads to remove dust, dirt and grime build-up. Be sure to clean under hold-down straps.

Cleaning

Most seats feature a plastic base on the bottom, to which the pad is attached and hinges or mounts secured. This plastic base is also equipped with holes that expose a foam pad. To avoid soaking the pad, use the least amount of water possible when cleaning the base. Use a paintbrush or toothbrush to dislodge dirt stuck around upholstery ends, hinges, screws and so on. For the most part, this base will only be dusty. The majority of time, cleaning is accomplished with a damp towel or wash mitt. Thoroughly dry the seat with a clean towel.

Many touring bikes feature large, soft seats with tucks, buttons and creases. Before washing, vacuum lint and dust from tucks and under buttons using the crevice tool attachment on a vacuum cleaner. This will reduce the amount of residue created during the wash.

120

If the seat is not in bad shape, soiled mainly with light dust, there is no reason to aggressively scrub it with a heavy-duty cleaner and brush. However, if it is embedded with dirt, don't hesitate to scrub with a soft brush and cleaner. Make sure cleaner residue is thoroughly rinsed from creases and folds.

Seat hinges tend to collect dust and dirt, and should be washed with a paintbrush and/or toothbrush. Vigorous cleaning will remove lubrication, so plan to treat hinges with a light coat of WD-40, white lithium grease or other lubricant after the bike has been washed and dried.

Conditioning

Applying vinyl dressing to seats causes the same concern as dressing on foot rubbers and handgrips. A slippery motorcycle seat is not conducive to safe riding. The best way to keep motorcycle seats looking good is to protect them from the sun. If the bike has to be parked outdoors, put a cover over it. Barring that, park it in the shade.

On a rare occasion, you may feel compelled to apply a light coat of dressing to a weathered seat. Such an instance may be during the initial detail of a used and neglected bike you just purchased. If this is the case, wash the bike, dry it off, apply dressing and let it soak in overnight. Then, wash the bike again the next day. Be certain the seat is thoroughly washed with lots of soap and water. Continue to wash and dry the seat until the surface no longer feels slippery.

Leather seats

Leather seats require the same kind of cleaning as vinyl but with different cleaning and condition-

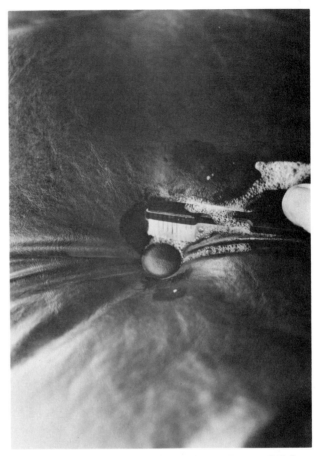

Buttons on saddle seats collect a lot of dust and debris under them. Use a soft toothbrush to dislodge dirt and scrub away build-up. The crevice attachment on a vacuum cleaner also works well to remove this kind of debris.

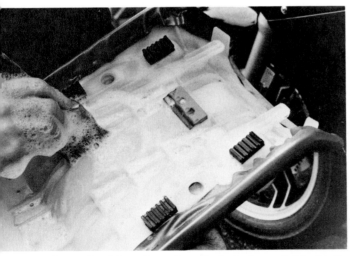

The undersides of most seats include a rigid plastic base. Clean this with a minimal amount of soapsuds and a toothbrush. Holes in the base expose the seat's thick foam pad. Too much water soaking into the pad may lead to mildew or rot problems.

Embedded dirt on vinyl seats is lightly scrubbed clean with a plastic-bristled brush. For the most part, ordinary wash soap and water work fine. For tough stains, use cleaner with the brush.

ing products. Leather needs to breathe, an attribute that helps to make them so comfortable. Using a harsh cleaner may fade the lustrous shine, and using an inappropriate dressing or wax will clog the pores and reduce its breathing ability. Use products especially made for leather care, such as Harley-Davidson Leather Care, Lexol and Hide Food.

Cleaning

Initial cleaning may consist of vacuuming lint from seams, creases and beads. Use a clean wash mitt rinsed with clear water to remove dust and light dirt. More stubborn stains may require the use of Leather Care or other leather cleaning product along with some mild scrubbing with a soft toothbrush.

A gentle washing with car wash soap and water is safe for most leather seats as long as you don't get too carried away with vigorous scrubbing. Dampen a wash mitt in a bucket of fresh wash soap and wring out excess water. Then, bring up a mittful of foam to wash away light films of road dirt. Rinse with clear water and dry. If dirt still persists, opt for a leather cleaning product like Lexol instead of using a cleaner. Lexol is designed to clean leather and will not remove the oils needed to preserve it. Apply as directed using a soft, clean cloth or towel. Buff off residue with a clean cloth.

Conditioning

After cleaning a leather seat, always apply a thin coat of leather conditioner to the surface. Leather Care is a one-step product designed to

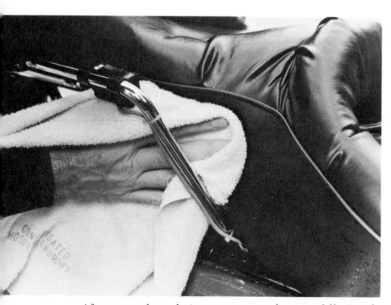

After a wash and rinse, water tends to puddle inside folds and tucks on saddle seats. Use a thick towel to dry the seat and also wipe off surrounding parts, such as brackets and armrests. A fold in the towel is used to reach along seams, beads and around buttons.

clean, polish and preserve with each application. Lexol manufactures a cleaner and a separate conditioner to be applied after cleaning. Regardless of the product you use, be sure a conditioner is included in the process or applied afterward to help preserve the natural oils in the leather. Application is made with a soft cloth. Allow conditioner to dry and then buff off residue with a clean cloth.

Waterproofing and protecting

The label on Leather Care also states that this product leaves behind a water repellent finish. This is important to motorcycle riders who occasionally get caught in the rain. Other products also contain water repellent features and you should read the labels to ensure they have this quality. Water saturation into leather seats will eventually dry the material and cause it to crack or tear. Optimum leather care requires the material to be clean, conditioned and water resistant.

The sun is a natural enemy to leather, just as it is to vinyl. The best protection is afforded when the bike is parked in a covered garage. If it has to be parked for long periods in the sun, consider covering the seat with a large towel or using a quality motorcycle cover that breathes. Other than that, attempt to park in a shaded area, or, at least alternate parking positions so that one part of the seat is not consistently facing the sun. You may choose to park the bike with the front wheel toward the front of a parking stall one day and then back it in the next.

You should also make sure the leather seat is rich with conditioner if it is to be subjected to the sun's rays for extended periods. The sun will dry out leather and rob the seat of the oils it needs to stay rich and pliable.

Saddlebags

It used to be that only the big "hog" riders and motorcycle policemen rode motorcycles with saddlebags. The rest of us would get along by stuffing carry-on baggage under our shirts or jackets. Nowadays, we are much more practical and understand the convenience of saddlebags. Daily commuters can pack away briefcases and a lunch, and weekend travelers can stow plenty of clothes and goodies. Keeping saddlebags clean will help the entire bike look good, and keeping them leak free will help to preserve the stuff you put in them.

Soft-sided bags

Many motorcycle shops offer soft-sided saddlebags, tank packs and fanny packs. These handy bags are generally made of a lightweight synthetic material which is durable and easy to clean. Adjustable straps allow tank packs and saddlebags to fit on most motorcycles and fanny packs are designed to be worn like a belt around your waist.

If specific washing and drying methods are required, instructions will be found on a label sewn onto the bag, generally on an inside seam. In the absence of such instructions, you can safely use water and a mild liquid soap to remove dirt and stains. Extra-dirty bags can be washed in a sink, rinsed with clear water and then hung outside or above a bathtub to air dry. Soft-sided bags and packs with built-in foam dividers or reinforcements should

not be subjected to drenching in a sink of water. For those, use a sponge to apply soapy foam for cleaning and a soft brush as needed for scrubbing. Towel dry as best you can and then hang the bag from a coat hanger in the bathtub to air dry completely.

Bug residue is removed with a toothbrush and dirt build-up is quickly removed from flaps and seams with a paintbrush. If the bag was subjected to wet-weather riding and is covered with a gritty road film, brush off the debris with a paintbrush or soft plastic brush before washing. This will remove most of the film and prevent grit from getting on the zipper during the wash.

Plastic zippers are common on soft-sided bags and packs. Most of them are protected by a flap and some of the flaps are secured with Velcro. This helps to keep the bags sealed and protect items carried inside. Should the zipper be subjected to dust and dirt, use a toothbrush to clean between the teeth and along the seam. Rinse with clear water

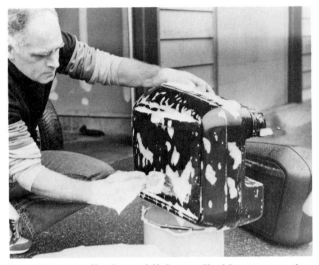

Rory Vance pulls the saddlebags off of his Katana for washing. To prevent scratches, he sets the bags on top of a plastic wash bucket instead of the bare ground. Having the bags off the ground also makes them easier to handle during the wash.

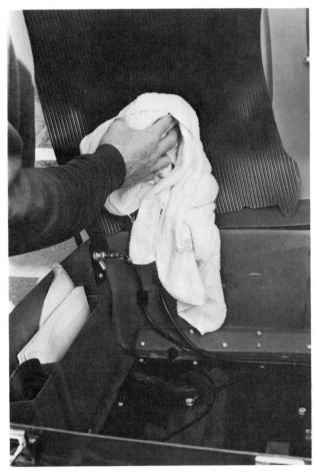

With vinyl saddlebags off the bike, they can be heavily sprayed with dressing without an overspray problem. Once a year is about right for heavy saddlebag dressing applications. Use a clean paintbrush to work dressing into the texture and seams. Buff off excessive dressing with a dressing cloth. Use folds in the cloth to remove dressing from seams and grooves. For spiffs, apply dressing to the cloth first and then wipe on.

Inside portions of saddlebags rarely need more than a wipedown with a damp cloth, depending on what was carried in them. Once a year, or as often as needed, use a towel sprayed with cleaner to remove accumulations of dirt. In the corners, you may need to use a paintbrush or toothbrush to dislodge build-up.

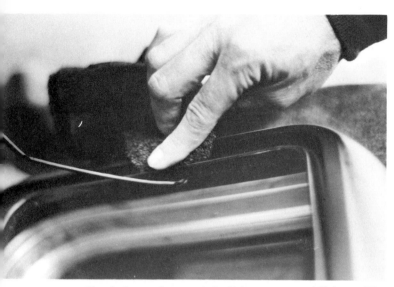

Check the seal around the lid cover on saddlebags. Dirt or other build-up can cause a break in the seal and result in water leaks and excessive dust exposure. Use a toothbrush or the fold of a towel for cleaning.

and allow to air dry. Lubricate zippers as they become stiff to operate. Refrain from using liquid lubricants and choose instead to apply a dry stick lubricant. The dry lubricant will not attract dust like

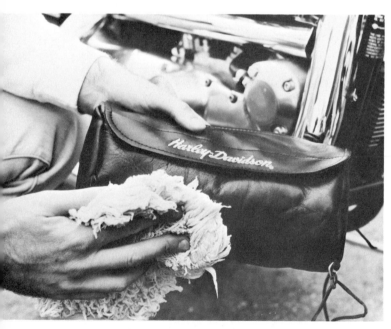

Remove leather saddlebags and other leather accessories before washing your motorcycle, there is no need to get them unnecessarily wet. The leather fork bag on Dan Mycon's Sportster was splattered with bug residue. It is cleaned with a damp wash mitt and clear water. Use cleaner only as necessary to remove stubborn build-up.

a liquid, which will help to keep the bag and its contents cleaner.

Rigid vinyl bags

Rory Vance has rigid vinyl saddlebags on his Suzuki Katana. He likes them because they hold a lot, are quickly removed from the bike by way of a key lock and include a nifty handle, just like a suitcase.

To wash the bags, Vance removes them from the bike. Rather than setting them directly on the ground, he prefers to rest them on top of a plastic bucket to prevent scratches while washing. They can also be laid on top of a towel or other soft surface for scratch prevention. Normal wash soap and water are generally sufficient for most cleaning needs. Vance uses a paintbrush to dislodge grit caught in the metal support band and a toothbrush to remove stubborn bug residue.

The most troublesome detailing problem he has had with these vinyl saddlebags is scuff marks made from his boot when he gets on and off the bike. Art Wentworth believes a consistent coat of vinyl dressing maintained on top of the bags will help reduce the degree to which scuff marks mar the vinyl. He figures dressing will keep that part of the saddlebag slippery and therefore allow the boot to slip over the surface rather than scuff it. Since overspray is not a problem, while the bags are off the bike, they can be sprayed with vinyl dressing and then buffed with a cloth. For spiffs, spray the cloth and then apply to the bag.

Cleaning the inside of rigid vinyl saddlebags is done with a vacuum cleaner and damp wash mitt. Unless you spill something inside them, stains will not be a problem. In lieu of a vacuum cleaner, use a paintbrush to sweep loose debris from the inside of the bags. It is also a good idea to check the condition of seals and gaskets around the openings of these saddlebags. A stubborn deposit of dirt could prevent a tight seal when the bag is closed, which would permit dust or water to enter the inside of the bag and soil its contents.

Leather bags

For optimum cleaning and conditioning results on leather saddlebags, use the cleaning and conditioning products recommended by the manufacturer or supplier of the saddlebags. This is by far the safest way to maintain quality leather accessories.

Harley-Davidson shop owner Peter Danikas carries Harley-Davidson's Leather Care and recommends its use on the leather bags sold from his store. Other leather care products are available at auto parts stores. Lexol Cleaner works well to clean leather and remove stains, and Lexol and Hide Food are recommended for quality leather conditioning.

There is no reason to use a lot of water while cleaning leather saddlebags; soaking the material will merely add to the required drying time. Instead, brush off accumulated grit and sand with a soft paintbrush. Then, use a soft cloth dampened with your choice of leather cleaner. If necessary, scrub with a toothbrush to remove stubborn build-up and debris.

After cleaning, always treat leather bags with a light coat of leather conditioner. Cleaning causes the removal of certain oils that could eventually dry out leather, making it susceptible to cracks and tears. No matter which cleaning or conditioning product you use, always follow directions on the label to make sure you use the proper application technique.

Although products are made to protect leather from water, there are times when leather saddlebags suffer a complete drenching. For leather saddlebags that are completely soaked by rain-flooded highways, it won't hurt to rinse them off with clear water to remove grit and sand. If, on the other hand, they are only damp, opt to let them dry before cleaning and conditioning.

Art Wentworth has had good results stuffing wet leather saddlebags with newspaper and then placing them on thick towels close to a heater or other warm, dry location. Newspaper helps the inside to dry by absorbing water and moisture from the leather. Check the newspaper occasionally for dampness, as you might have to insert dry newspaper after only a few hours. The bags may have to sit overnight before they dry completely. When dry, use a soft paintbrush to remove encrusted grit and sand. You may need a toothbrush in seams and tight corners. Follow that with a treatment of cleaner, as needed, and then conditioner.

Pitted and discolored chrome

Chrome becomes pitted through neglect and prolonged exposure to harsh substances, like exhaust vapors and salt water. The only way to totally restore pitted chrome is to have the damaged piece professionally rechromed. To extend the life of chrome and prevent the formation of pitted rust spots, you should maintain a frequent washing and waxing schedule. Once a month is not too often to wax chrome pieces when a motorcycle is constantly parked close to salt water and an atmosphere laden with moist salt water sea breezes.

Pitted chrome can be detailed to look better, but by no means as permanently as new chrome. Bright silver paint is used to touch up pits. Close inspection will reveal the alteration, but from a distance, the repair is hardly noticeable.

A damaged spot must be thoroughly cleaned with soap and water and an SOS pad. Remove as much dirt discoloration as possible without peeling off additional flakes of chrome. Rinse the spot

with water and dry. Wipe the spot again with a dab of paint thinner or Prepsol on a cloth to be sure it is totally clean. Allow the spot to dry completely.

Use a fine artist's paintbrush or the bottom of a paper matchstick to apply bright silver paint to the blemish. Two light coats are better than a single heavy one. Take your time and paint only the pits, not the surrounding chrome. Rest your hand against the bike for support and added control.

Rubber parts

Besides footpeg rubbers and handgrips, there are a number of various rubber parts on a motorcycle. Fuel tanks are mounted on rubber bushings, taillights are mounted on rubber gaskets and, of course, the tires are rubber. Cleaning is accomplished with soap and water. At times, it may be necessary to scrub with a brush and cleaner.

Extra-dirty rubber pieces may require the cleaning strength of a powdered cleanser and scrub brush. Most likely, those pieces would be foot rubbers and tires. Time, patience and elbow grease are the key here. Rubber parts painted with tire black

You can never go wrong using a conditioning product specifically made for the leather equipment on your motorcycle. Harley-Davidson recommends Leather Care for use on their leather saddlebags and seats.

Dressing vinyl and rubber parts sandwiched between metal pieces is a difficult chore. To make the job easier on a relatively clean motorcycle, dress these parts first using a paintbrush. Excess dressing is removed with soapsuds and a paintbrush. The rubber gasket between the two will maintain enough dressing to keep it looking good, even after the wash.

look altered. It is much better to spend extra time cleaning than to hide stains and embedded dirt under a layer of cosmetic cover-up.

Small rubber parts like fuel tank bushings and tool kit straps are removed and cleaned in the wash

Polish and wax residue in the joint between the mirror mount and housing is removed with a few whisks of a paintbrush. More stubborn build-up may require the strength of a toothbrush.

bucket. Use a toothbrush and cleaner as necessary. Be sure to clean bushing mounts and tool kits, too.

Dressing rubber parts with Armor All or other polypenetrant is a subject of concern. Most motorcycle enthusiasts believe dressing causes rubber parts to become slippery, which may be a hazard while operating the machine. They prefer to keep foot rubbers and handgrips free of dressing, opting to clean them more often to maintain a like-new appearance.

One exception to dressing foot rubbers and handgrips may be the once-a-year detail, when those parts are really starting to look dry and weathered. Art Wentworth and Ralph Maughn have done this to their bikes on rare occasion. They wash the bike first and dry it. Then, they apply a good coat of dressing on dried rubber parts and work it in with a paintbrush. Dressing is allowed to soak in for a few hours, sometimes overnight. Afterward, the entire motorcycle is thoroughly washed again with soap and water.

The extended amount of time that dressing was allowed to soak in, and the following thorough wash, combined to remove the slippery aftereffect of dressing application. Rejuvenation of the rubber parts was achieved because silicones had a chance to sink deep into the rubber. Excessive surface dressing residue was washed off, leaving the surface of those rubber parts relatively dry and not slippery.

Cleaning other rubber pieces is accomplished in much the same fashion. Thin edges of rubber gaskets and cushions are scrubbed with a toothbrush. Dressing these edges, especially when they are located between two painted pieces, is accomplished in one of two ways.

On a relatively clean motorcycle, you may choose to dress these parts before washing the bike. Use a paintbrush to work dressing into the piece and achieve complete coverage. Don't worry about overspray or smears on paint or chrome surfaces. After everything has been dressed to your satisfaction, wash the motorcycle with plenty of soap and water. This removes overspray and smears from paint and chrome, as well as excess dressing from the rubber parts. Rubber will look clean and fresh and not sport the super-glossy appearance so common with excessive dressing application.

Another way to apply dressing on thin rubber pieces sandwiched between non-rubber surfaces is with a cotton swab. This is a meticulous method and much more time consuming than the one just described. About the only time an enthusiast may employ this method is for touch-up just before a motorcycle show. Spray the swab with dressing, or, dip an end into the bottle. Squeeze out excess with your fingers. Lay a soft cloth on the bike and rest your hand on it for steady application. The cloth will prevent oils on your hand from smearing paint or chrome.

Vinyl parts

Vinyl tank pads, fender moldings, light housings and saddlebags are all washed with soap and water. By far, the most common mistake made by novice enthusiasts and detailers is smearing polish and wax on vinyl. Ordinary washing with soap and water will not remove polish or wax residue from textured vinyl. It will require the scrubbing strength of a soft brush and cleaner.

Art Wentworth's 1985 Suzuki GS 1150 E features rear turn signal lights encased in a rigid vinyl assembly. One of the lights was inadvertently scraped against a piece of painted wood trim, resulting in paint impregnating the case. Truly an eyesore, Wentworth used an SOS pad to gently scrub the spot. Paint was soon removed, and a light application of dressing made the light look new.

Don't be afraid to clean vinyl. As with painted pieces, start out by using the mildest cleaning method first, like car wash soap and a wash mitt. Then, gradually increase cleaning strength by employing cleaner and a toothbrush. As a last resort, use an SOS pad. If you are concerned that a certain cleaning method may be too abrasive or harsh for a particular piece, clean an inconspicuous part of the bike first that is made of the same material. If the result is less than satisfactory, no harm will be done. By the same token, don't immediately start heavy scrubbing on any part with a brush, SOS pad

or other abrasive. Always start out gently, with a light touch. Detailing requires thoughtful consideration not only for thorough cleaning but also for overall vehicle preservation.

Most vinyl is dressed with good results. As with seats, foot rubbers and handgrips, it is recommended you consider what you plan to dress and just what role that part plays in the operation and control of the machine. Light cases, fender moldings and the like sustain an improved appearance with a light application of vinyl dressing. Best results are accomplished by spraying dressing on the dressing cloth and then wiping it onto the vinyl surface. Use your finger inside the cloth to maintain control of the application and keep dressing off of chrome and painted parts.

Mirrors and headlight lenses

The glass on motorcycle mirrors seldom requires much more than a swipe with the wash mitt. To help mirrors look crisp, use a floppy paintbrush around it in the space between the glass and the mirror housing. Much of the time, dust collects in this space and is not washed away with just the efforts of the wash mitt.

Severely stained mirrors that refuse to sparkle after repeated applications of the wash mitt may require the strength of a glass cleaner. Once in a while, a mirror has been so badly neglected that it requires the use of #0000 steel wool and glass cleaner combined. That maneuver should be followed with another wash mitt application and a thorough rinse with clear water, in order to remove all traces of steel wool fibers.

The mark at the top right corner of this side light is a paint smudge. The light was knocked against a piece of wood trim, resulting in paint rubbing off onto the vinyl cover. Careful light scrubbing with a wet SOS pad quickly removed the blemish.

After the paint smudge was removed, a light coat of Armor All was applied to the vinyl surface. Excess was buffed off, and the light looked new again.

It is best to remove the spare tire for detailed washing and cleaning of the trailer. The wheel and tire should also be washed, with the tire dressed and the rim polished and waxed on both sides. Then drop the tongue support on motorcycle trailers for detailed cleaning. A paintbrush works great for reaching tight spaces and dislodging dirt and accumulations of road debris.

Glass headlight lenses, as well as other glass light lenses, suffer the effects of bug residue time after time. On long trips, it may not be feasible to clean the headlight every hundred miles. Therefore, residue becomes encrusted and difficult to remove.

Start out with soap and water. Sometimes, water will soak into the residue and loosen it up. Many times, a few flicks with your fingernail is all

Don Perry is using a paint block while touching up a small paint flaw on the frame of his trailer. Paint blocks are used on wide open areas such as frames and trailer tongues because there are not many obstacles in the way. The bottom of a shoe box makes a perfect paint block.

it takes to remove the residue. For those extra-stubborn episodes, you will eventually have to resort to #0000 steel wool and glass cleaner. Art Wentworth has also had luck using #0000 steel wool and a one-step liquid wax. Suffice to say, it is best to use a liquid along with steel wool to reduce the scratch hazard.

Motorcycle trailers

Don Perry and his wife Mary have put nearly 60,000 miles on their 1980 Honda Gold Wing Interstate in just eight years. Well versed in motorcycle touring, they like the advantages a motorcycle trailer has to offer. You would be amazed at the number of items they can fit into this handy little unit.

Trailer detailing is no different than for motorcycles. The surface area is easier to reach, and consists mainly of a painted body, tongue, wheels and tires. For best access to underside areas, remove the spare tire and let down the tongue support. Like on a motorcycle, clean the axle and underside first while the ground is dry. Use a paintbrush and plastic brush as needed to remove accumulations of dirt and grime. Use an old wash mitt on this area since it may be quite encrusted with road debris, such as tar and oil.

A paintbrush works well to clean tight areas along the tongue and trailer hitch. It is also useful on wheels, around taillights and along the seam between the lid and trailer body. Wash the trailer with a clean wash mitt and a bucket of fresh soapy wash water. Apply the mitt in a straight back-and-forth pattern to avoid swirls. Rinse frequently to prevent soap or water from drying on paint.

Twice a year, more if you prefer, pull the hubcaps off of the trailer wheels. Thoroughly clean the wheel and the inside of the hubcap. Later, when the trailer is dry, plan to polish and wax the wheel and hubcap. This is also an opportune time to check the torque on lug nuts.

Polish and wax techniques are the same for the trailer as for the motorcycle. The type of polish used on the trailer will depend on the degree of oxidation and severity of scratch blemishes. Chrome is cared for with Simichrome or chrome polish of choice.

Minor paint work is done on the frame, axle and tongue with a spray can. The need for masking should be minimal, as a paint block made from a thin piece of cardboard works fine. The size and thickness of the bottom of a shoe box makes a perfect paint block. Painted wheels can be repainted without removing the tire. They should be pulled off of the trailer for ease of application. Carefully mask the tire with masking tape and use a paint block to prevent overspray problems. Should paint get on the tire, use a dab of lacquer thinner on a rag to remove.

Chapter 10

Final inspection

Two days can easily be spent on an annual detail: one day dedicated to cleaning, the other to polishing, waxing and getting things right. Ralph Maughn and Steve Jacobs turn annual details into winter projects, sometimes taking weeks to dismantle, clean, paint, polish, wax and totally service their motorcycles in preparation for the next riding season or Baja trip.

No matter how much time you allocate to detailing, the job is not complete until a final inspection is made. After spending hours cleaning and shining, you owe it to yourself to go over the bike one last time to ensure perfection.

Sunlight inspection

Under artificial light, your motorcycle may look absolutely stunning. That is because most light bulbs do not create enough brilliance to illuminate minute spider webbing and tiny spots of dirt. Bright sunlight, on the other hand, is unforgiving. In sunlight, you will quickly spot blemishes, smears and other detail imperfections.

Grab a clean cloth, cut-off paintbrush and the dressing cloth. Pull your bike out into the sunlight and park it in a convenient location. Plan a systematic front-to-back, top-to-bottom and side-to-side search for anything that needs attention.

Look for wax build-up, smears, spider webbing, paint chips, dust, dirt, grease, inconsistent dressing applications, missed chrome and the like. You should also check for loose screws, bolts, nuts, cables, hand levers, wheels and chain adjusters. You can even go a meticulous step further and align screw heads so they all point in the same direction.

As the inspection continues, you may find yourself looking at a side of your motorcycle away

The back end of this Electra Glide is in great need of a wash, wax and detail. Hours will be spent cleaning the motorcycle, using paintbrushes and toothbrushes to remove dirt and road grime from intricate places like light assemblies, brackets and trim.

A lot of time was taken to make this bike look new again, using only cleaning and polishing supplies. A detailer owes it to him or herself to go over the bike a final time in sunlight to search for any detail missed areas for perfection.

129

Sunlight is unforgiving. Under a light bulb, a motorcycle may look great. Out in the sun, though, you will notice wax and dressing smears, dirt tucked away in corners and other minor imperfections.

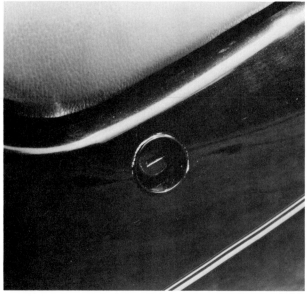

Wax build-up around this key slot is removed with a cut-off paintbrush and then buffed with a soft cloth. Removing this kind of minor oversight will make your bike look crisp.

from the sun. Shadows cast on that side will make it tough to spot dirt and other imperfections. Take a minute to reposition the bike so that side faces the sun. Employ whatever means necessary to achieve a perfect detail, even going so far as to use a cotton swab to remove small accumulations of debris from deep inside engine fins.

Handlebar and instrument area

Last-minute detailing may entail some wax build-up removal and other cleaning projects that could produce dust debris. For that reason, you should start the inspection at the top of the bike and work down. As dust or lint is dislodged, it will fall to lower parts of the bike and be cleaned when you get to that area.

Check mirror faces for smears and water spots. Look at the edge between the glass and mirror housing. Dust in that area is swept away with a dry paintbrush. Look at both ends of the mirror support and remove any lingering build-up next to the locking nut or swivel base.

Handgrips must be clean. If they were treated with dressing, be sure all excess is wiped off and the surface is free of any slippery feeling. Dust and minor build-up around turn-signal switches and horn buttons is quickly cleaned with the cut-off paintbrush. Getting rid of debris in these areas makes them look crisp and new. Continue inspecting the handlebars to be sure they are shiny and smear-free. Do the same to the triple clamp, using a paintbrush to whisk away dust and lint.

Instrument clusters must sport an evenly balanced dressing application. In the sunlight, you will notice any spot that was not touched with the dressing cloth. Having used the same cloth for all dressing needs, there should be enough dressing left on it for minor touch-up. Be sure instrument faces are not smeared and cables are neatly routed.

Both sides of the windshield ought to be clear and spot-free. Minor scratches are rubbed out with plastic polish. Check mounting bracket bases for wax residue and screw heads for cleanliness. Use the cut-off paintbrush as needed and wipe off residue with a soft clean cloth.

The headlight assembly received a lot of attention during the initial wash and subsequent detailing. Be certain wax was not left in the gap around the trim ring. Use the correct tool to check the tightness of screws, aligning them as you see fit. Extend this concentrated examination to other light assemblies around the headlight, including fog lights and turn signals.

Openly mounted instruments, like the speedometer on Dan Mycon's Sportster and odometer on Ralph Maughn's Yamaha, must have clear lens faces, clean bodies and tidy cable connections. Use a toothbrush to remove wax or dust build-up on threaded cable stems and trim rings. Survey the condition of screws at the bottom of these gauges to be sure they are dirt-free and adequately secured.

Fuel tank and seat

A few large touring bikes feature gauges and switches mounted on the fuel tank. Give them the same attention you would other gauges, switches and key ignitions. The tank itself should be free of spider webbing, wax build-up and smears. Meguiar's #7 or similar polish will erase imperfections and leave the paint swirl-free and bursting with color. Apply a light coat of wax afterward for long-lasting protection.

Inspect the seat for cleanliness. If dressing was applied, be sure excess is buffed off and the texture not slippery. Open seats to inspect the area underneath. Look for dust and dirt on the battery and top of the rear fender. Don't forget the actual seat bottom and hinges.

Large seats with buttons and tucks are thoroughly examined by stretching the material to open creases. You will be surprised at how much dust and lint accumulates under buttons and deep inside creases. Pull up seat flaps to track down dirt on the back of the flaps and those areas covered by them. Let no space go untouched.

Sissy bars and the seats and bags attached to them are scrutinized for shine and wax residue. Unique designs built into sissy bars may call for the use of cotton swabs to remove dust and debris from intricate valleys and recesses. Look over support brackets and mounting bolts for dirt in seams and along edges.

Top-mounted rear fender tour-paks may be dusty. Wipe them off with a soft, clean cotton cloth. Insert the cloth through luggage racks, and hold an end in each hand with the rack in the middle. Move your hands back and forth to buff the underside of rack brackets. The cut-off paintbrush will dislodge wax build-up around mounting brackets. Open the tour-pak box to be sure it is clean inside. Also, look for polish and/or wax build-up along the edge of the lid and body, as well as the locking mechanism.

At this point, the top of your motorcycle should be as near perfect as possible. I realize you can literally spend days looking for and removing dirt from such out-of-the-way spaces as cable ends on hand levers. It goes without saying that the closer you look, the more imperfections you will find. This kind of scrutiny is good, and you can take it as far as you want.

Preparing a motorcycle for a show demands scrupulous attention to every minute detail, in some cases calling for complete restoration. This

Inspect mirrors and look for wax build-up in lettering and smears on glass. Leftover wax around the Suzuki lettering on this mirror housing should have been removed with a toothbrush during the initial wash.

Vance was surprised to find the inside portion of Allen head screws on the motorcycle's body starting to rust out, just like those on the fuel tank. The screw heads were cleaned and painted with bright silver paint to make them look new and prevent future rust problems. The reason some of the Allen head screws were rusting on Vance's bike was because protective plastic inserts had vibrated loose and fallen out. After the detail, he went to the Suzuki shop and bought new inserts.

intense attention to detail is expected if one hopes to compete for first-place honors. For the everyday driver, however, this kind of attention may be given only once a year. Because of the extended amount of time between complete details, it is important to cover every square inch of the motorcy-

cle to ensure its operation and appearance longevity.

Fairing

Motorcycle fairings come in basically two styles: the full wraparound sport type, and the two-piece fork and frame-mounted kind found on touring bikes. On touring bikes, the upper fairing is checked out along with the handlebars and windshield, while the lower section is inspected with the engine.

Full fairings on sport bikes have to be off the bike in order to get to the engine. After engine work is complete and you are completely satisfied with the results, clean, polish and wax the fairing before putting it back on the bike.

A final inspection of fairings consists mainly of looking for paint flaws, such as hairline scratches, swirls and spider webbing. Look for wax residue in seams and screw heads; use the cut-off paintbrush and a clean cloth to spruce them up.

Rory Vance was surprised to find rust starting inside the heads of Allen head screws along the side of the fairing and frame on his Katana. The heads were cleaned and then painted with bright silver paint, just like those on the fuel cap assembly. Rust got a start because plastic caps originally placed on the screw heads had vibrated loose and fallen out. After the detail, Vance bought and installed new caps to prevent the problem from recurring.

The lower front sections of fairings suffer the most wear and tear because of road hazards thrown up by the front wheel. Provide extra protection for

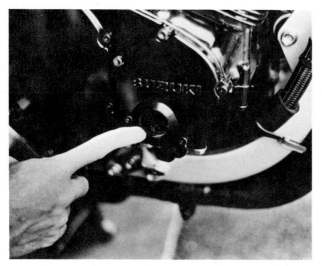

The wear mark on this side plate was caused from chafing by the lower fairing on Rory Vance's Katana. The cause of the problem was not related to a broken or misaligned part. New paint would just be rubbed off again, so Vance opted to cover this piece with black electrician's tape.

Tidy strips of electrician's tape protect the side plate and will cushion future chafing from the fairing. During the next detail, or the next time the fairing is removed, these strips should be checked and replaced if necessary.

this area by neatly applying strips of black electrician's tape on the lower surface. Depending on the color of your fairing, these strips may not be noticed.

Additionally, there may be spots on engine cases that are susceptible to prolonged vibration and chafing by the fairing, which results in wear marks. Essentially, paint on the cases is rubbed off. To prevent further wear, spots are touched up with the right paint and then covered with black electrician's tape applied in neat strips. Of course, if wear marks are due to a broken mount or other damaged or misaligned part, make the necessary repairs to prevent future problems.

Scrapes and scratches on fairings are touched up just like other painted pieces. Touch-up paint is available at the motorcycle shop. Minor cracks and slight damage to fairings as a result of a fall or collision may be repairable. Since all fairings are neither constructed with identical materials nor manufacturing techniques, I recommend you allow a professional auto body shop to make the repairs. If the fairing has suffered severe damage, you should replace it with a new one.

Front wheel

Continue from where you left off at the bottom of the headlight assembly. Check the fork tubes and seals for missed debris and build-up on seal edges. On the fork tubes, are there any paint chips? How about dirt build-up on the axle bolts and fender mounts? Does paint on the fender look right? What about wax on reflectors, emblems and vinyl moldings?

Hunt for imperfections on cables and brake assemblies. Use a paintbrush, toothbrush and cut-off brush as necessary to remove dust and build-up. Rotate the wheel to allow access to holes and slots on brake discs. You may have to utilize a cotton swab to wipe away dust in these slots.

Scan the wheel rim for dressing smears. Give the axle housing the once-over and survey the condition of spokes and nipples. Once again, detail brushes and a soft clean cloth are your best tools. Polish and wax as you see fit to maintain a consistent finish on chrome and alloy wheels. Touch up paint chips as called for and lightly treat rubber valve stems with dressing.

Tires require a uniform application of dressing on the upper sidewalls. Dull whitewalls and those displaying a bluish tint from excessive dressing are brightened with the edge of a dry SOS pad. Continue to rotate the wheel and inspect it until you are satisfied that both sides are as clean and tidy as they can be.

Engine

Engines on full-fairing sport bikes can be detailed only with the lower fairing removed. Before replacing the fairing, be sure to give the engine a thorough inspection.

Start at the front of the engine. How does the top end look? Are fins clean and debris-free? If not, use a cotton swab or the handle of a toothbrush inserted into a clean cloth to wipe clean. Exhaust pipe engine connections should be clean, as well as the nuts and bolts that hold them in place. Bare spots on painted pipes are touched up with heat-resistant paint. Is the frame in need of polish or paint touch-up?

Examine the front of the engine and all of the pieces that are located there. Then, move over to one side of the engine. Again, start at the top and work down. Aggressive cleaning and attention to detail has probably left this area in good shape. Black crinkle-type paint on some engines may suffer chips or peeling. This kind of paint is available at motorcycle shops and should be used for touch-up. Other than that, you may notice a few water spots that are wiped away with a damp cloth. Bill Buckingham uses long cotton swabs, like those found in a doctor's office, to reach residue deep inside valleys on lower ends just below the carburetors. You can find this sort of cotton swab at medical supply stores and pharmacies.

Work your way down the side of the engine to the bottom. There, check the skid plate and frame for dirt, grease and paint problems. Inspect footpegs and platforms, shift and brake levers, highway pegs, kickstand and kick starter. Use the right tools to check torque on screws and bolts, replacing any that have disappeared.

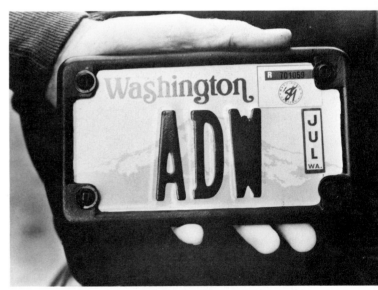

Screws can be added to the empty bottom holes of license plates to match those on top. Art Wentworth's personalized license plate is crisp-looking, uniform and balanced. He prefers to use plastic nuts and bolts because they will not rust and discolor.

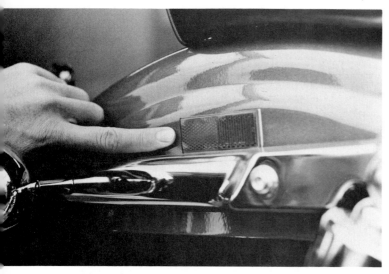

The reflector, bracket and fender on this motorcycle look crisp as well. Be sure to remove any hint of wax build-up from reflector lettering and along brackets to make that part on your bike look this good.

Quite naturally, you can't examine both sides of the engine at the same time. Concentrate your efforts on one side and then the other. Don't move away from the engine until it has been looked over completely and has passed your rigid inspection.

Take care of anything that needs attention right away, before it slips your mind. It is frustrat-

ing to have to go back and polish something after you have put away all of your detailing tools and supplies. If you took pictures of your motorcycle before detailing, use them as a cross-reference to ensure that parts were replaced correctly and areas needing special attention were taken care of.

Rear wheel

The same basic final inspection criteria used on the front wheel holds true for the rear one. In addition, you must check the chain and its need for lubrication and tightening, and examine sprocket teeth for wear.

Look at the chain guard for smears or blemishes and check mounts for loose nuts, bolts and screws. The swing arm may need a paint chip or two touched up, as well as the frame. Wipe off dust on the exhaust pipes and make sure there is no carbon build-up on the tip. Scan the rear fender for imperfections and don't neglect the taillight and license plate, frame and bracket.

When the rear wheel area has passed inspection, you can replace saddlebags. Are mounts clean and securely fastened? Are the insides of saddlebags clean? How about reflectors, emblems and locking mechanisms? To prevent smears on painted saddlebags from the oils in your hands, pick up and handle the bags using a clean towel.

Part replacement

Throughout the course of the detail, you had the opportunity to take note of parts that were bro-

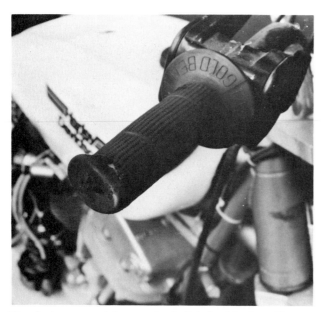

Handgrips cannot be repaired. It is best to install new ones if you want your motorcycle to look perfect. Other inexpensive parts suffering damage should also be replaced, such as footpeg rubbers, shift lever rubbers and mirrors.

Rory Vance lost a fairing screw during an extended road trip. It was replaced with a Phillips head screw, which does not match the remaining Allen head screws. The Phillips screw should be replaced with one that matches the rest for continuity and uniformity.

ken or worn. Damaged items such as handgrips and footpeg rubbers are inexpensive. They cannot be repaired and should therefore be replaced. The same holds true for cracked mirrors and instrument faces.

Even though Ralph Maughn's Baja trip was only 2,100 miles, a relatively short distance for touring motorcycles, his bike was subjected to some rough terrain and harsh environmental conditions. Before a drop of water was squirted on the bike, he had already made plans to replace a number of parts with new ones. He could have opted otherwise, but recognized the beating a dirt bike takes in comparison to one ridden strictly on pavement. In essence, his Yamaha TT 600 K was subjected to as much off-road riding in that one trip as other dirt bikes are subjected to in an entire riding season.

To ensure continued dependable and comfortable performance, Maughn bought new handgrips and protectors, rear tire, cables, front fender, fork tube boots, fork springs, steering bearing, chain guide and plastic side pieces. He was prepared to

A final inspection, and check with photographs taken before the detail, work as reminders to replace missing bolts, nuts and screws. Mechanical work should be done at this time while it is fresh on your mind.

Ralph Maughn's Yamaha looks pretty good after an extensive detail. There is some minor work left to be done, such as sprocket cleaning and chain and side stand in- *stallation. A plastic milk crate and a couple of two-by-fours worked out quite well as a support stand throughout the detail.*

Detailed cleaning of the back tire revealed a wear spot during the detail of Rory Vance's Katana. The groove on the center of the tire is supposed to be clear. The line next to Art Wentworth's finger is a wear indicator and signifies that the tire is ready for replacement.

buy new brake shoes but discovered the old ones were in excellent condition, showing only a surprisingly slight amount of dust and grit inside the drums. And to be on the safe side, he bought a new chain, although it wasn't really needed. Lubricating the chain every hundred miles or so paid off, as neither it nor the sprockets showed much sign of wear. Further service work included changing the engine oil and fork fluid.

The bike was initially washed after taking notes on what service needed to be performed and which parts had to be replaced. Thorough cleaning made dismantling easier, and also helped Maughn find pieces that were missing screws and damaged items that were not noticed earlier. Each part was

detailed as it came off the bike, which made reassembly quick and easy.

During the annual detail of his Katana, Rory Vance found a wear mark on the rear tire. This indicated that it was about time for a new one. He also found a screw missing on the fairing and some rust on tools in the tool kit.

Squire Tomasie can't afford to wait until season's end for complete detail and service work on his race bikes. His flat trackers are carefully cleaned and inspected after each event. To be a winner, he has to have a machine that will not break down. Part replacement is an ongoing segment of his detailing chores, justified by the serious nature of high-speed racing. I doubt anyone would feel comfortable riding a haphazardly maintained motorcycle while leaning it over and sliding through the curves of a racetrack at speeds near 100 miles per hour.

The degree to which you replace parts on your bike is up to your discretion and budget. It is fun to buy new motorcycle parts, but don't get too carried away. Conscientious service combined with considerate detailing will keep parts in good-looking and dependable condition.

Grand finale

Parked in the sunshine, a meticulously detailed motorcycle is truly a thing of beauty. The sparkle of bright chrome and depth of finely polished paint are accented by crisp black tires and glistening wheels.

Attention to detail is appreciated when notice is taken of polished light lenses and aligned screw heads. Emblems are sharp and clean, and easy to read and identify. The flawless windshield is almost invisible and the engine looks as if it has never been started. Your pride and joy, standing tall and ready to be admired by any passerby, has been detailed to perfection and probably looks better now than it did when you drove it off of the showroom floor.

Chapter 11

Rider accessories

Motorcycle riding is a pleasurable means of travel. Many enthusiasts depend on a motorcycle as their sole means of transportation, while it would seem that the majority like it because it's fun. Sitting on a bike with the wind in your face is an expression of freedom to many, epitomized by the old cliché, "You can always tell a happy motorcyclist by the amount of bugs in his teeth."

The design, performance and appearance of motorcycles has changed a lot over the years. So too, have the articles of clothing worn by the rider. Today, a number of states have enacted laws making helmets a mandatory accessory for every motorcycle rider. Granted, there are those who dispute these laws for one reason or another. But, helmets do serve a practical purpose and I'm sure are responsible for saving many lives. My recom-

mendation, and the recommendation of every enthusiast I have talked to, is to wear a helmet. It could make the difference between life and death, normal health and total paralysis.

Along with helmets, most serious motorcycle enthusiasts wear gloves, boots and leathers. This equipment not only keeps the rider warm and dry, but also serves as a skin-saving mechanism should the driver experience an unexpected fall. I don't know about you, but in my more youthful days I found out what pavement can quickly do to one's hide. Proudly sitting on my vintage Honda 305 Scrambler one sunny afternoon, oh so long ago, I decided to goose it and get sideways around a corner laced with just a bit of water and gravel. A quick twist of the throttle and a little lean into it got me sideways all right, clean down to the ground.

Just like in the movies, I found myself spread-eagle on the street with my bike ten yards ahead of

Helmet, goggles and gloves are minimum safety accessories that should be worn by all motorcyclists. This equipment belongs to Chris Shearer. His dad, Wally, won't let Chris ride the bike without them.

This is a sampling of Art Wentworth's rider accessories and the supplies he uses to clean and condition them. Alpinestars conditioner is used on the Alpinestars boots, and Langlitz Leather Conditioner on Langlitz leathers.

A soft toothbrush works well to remove bug residue from the grooves on helmets. In this instance, Art Wentworth is using a little one-step cleaner wax to help the toothbrush dislodge residue and further clean and shine the groove.

me screaming at full throttle. I jumped up and took care of the bike first, in true fashion, and then realized that my jeans were shredded, and half of the skin from my left leg was left embedded in the unforgiving asphalt, along with some hide from my hand and arm. I recovered fully, of course, but always wondered what a set of leathers and good gloves would have done for me.

Motorcycles offer no protection for the rider. Defensive driving must always be prevalent on the rider's mind, even in the dirt. Not only the roadways, but also the hills and deserts are rapidly becoming more crowded with motorcycle and ATV enthusiasts. Helmet, gloves, boots and leathers will protect you as best as anything can on a motorcycle. Conscientious upkeep of this equipment will not only help you to look your best while riding your machine, but also will play a significant role in the equipment's longevity.

Helmet

Helmets are subjected to rock chips, bug splatter, road tar and general dirt accumulation. Cleaning poses no big problem, it is just a matter of time and a little elbow grease. Basic cleaning consists of a wipedown with a damp wash mitt. Polishing is accomplished with the same products you used on your bike. If in doubt about product compatibility, test a spot on the helmet first before full application.

Most helmets are equipped with visor buttons or grooves around the face shield. Bug residue and dirt are removed from these areas with a toothbrush. You can also use the fold of a cloth to reach inside grooves to clean out accumulations of dust and lint. Additionally, a toothbrush works great for removing build-up along the edge of vinyl trim featured at the base.

Clear face shields are first cleaned with a wash mitt and clear water. Repeated applications of the mitt remove most bug residue. For stubborn spots, use plastic cleaner and polish, such as Meguiar's or Eagle 1. Plastic cleaner is designed to remove hairline scratches and other clarity blemishes. Plastic polish is much milder and should be used after an

A fold in the towel can be made to fit inside helmet grooves for cleaning. This also works well to remove water from the groove.

Clear face shields are wiped with a clean damp wash mitt or sponge. A sponge can be placed between the shield and helmet to reach inside the tight space between the top of the shield and the helmet.

138

application of cleaner, and on those clear shields that are only slightly blemished.

Dirty helmet straps are cleaned with soap and water. Use a toothbrush as needed to remove accumulations of dirt embedded in the weave. Pad the straps with a clean towel to absorb moisture and then allow to air dry.

A few motorcycle shops sell touch-up paint for helmets. Generally not a commonly stocked item, you may have to go to an auto body paint and supply store to have paint matched. Bottles of touch-up paint provide a brush attached to the cap. In lieu of that, use a fine artist's paintbrush or the clean end of a paper matchstick. Before painting, be sure the area around the chip is clean and free of wax or polish.

To keep a helmet in top shape, looking good and sparkling, you should occasionally polish and wax it. Art Wentworth prefers to use Meguiar's Car Cleaner Wax because it is a one-step product and does not leave a dry powdery residue. Any quality polish and wax will work fine, although you should follow the helmet manufacturer's product recommendations, if so provided.

Plastic cleaner and/or polish are used to remove hairline scratches and other minor blemishes on clear helmet shields. Apply in a straight back-and-forth pattern, as you would on painted motorcycle pieces.

Lenses on goggles are cleaned in a sink of warm soapy water and dried with a soft cloth. Severe scratches may not be easily removed by plastic polish and should be replaced. Motorcycle shops offer a variety of goggle sizes and styles, as well as other rider accessories.*

It is frustrating to get caught in the rain while out on a ride. Water spots on the visor add to the frustration. Rain-X is a product designed to quickly shed water. Applied to a helmet visor, it is supposed to keep water from beading, allowing clear vision through the shield. Dave Williams has had good results using Pledge Furniture Polish on his BMW helmet visor to shed water. If you have a favorite system for preventing water spots on your visor, use it, there is no reason to change.

Most of the time, except for dirt riders that fall down a lot, helmets are scratched and chipped while off of the rider's head. You may carefully set your helmet on the mirror of your bike, only to have the kids reach for it and knock it down. One of the best ways to keep your helmet protected while not wearing it is to place it in a helmet bag during non-use periods.

Dan Mycon has children and knows that his little guys would love to play with his Shoei hel-

met. He also knows what the helmet would look like after the boys played with it for any longer than two seconds. Therefore, he keeps his helmet in a soft storage bag in the closet, right above his leather riding gear.

Goggles

Although the use of goggles is not as popular today as it was a few years ago, quite a few motocross enthusiasts still prefer an open-faced helmet with visor and a pair of goggles for eye protection. Some riders, such as police officers, just wear sunglasses. Regardless of the type or style, eye protection is a definite must while operating a motorcycle. Anyone who has been blasted by a bug at highway speeds can attest to that.

Goggles are easy to clean. They are wiped off with a damp cloth or taken apart and washed with soap and water in the kitchen sink. Dry with a clean towel. After cleaning and drying, Wally Shearer buffs on a very light coat (less than half a drop) of liquid dish soap to the inside of goggle lenses to prevent them from fogging up. It works very well.

Scratches are removed with plastic cleaner and then finely buffed with plastic polish. Those lenses suffering severe scratches or cracks should be replaced. Various lenses are available at most motorcycle shops and some surplus stores. Although clear lenses are best for all-around riding, especially at night, you can purchase them in amber and dark "smoked" tints.

Gloves

Quality gloves are a mainstay for dirt and desert riders. Even if a dirt rider stays on his bike throughout the ride, he is subjected to hand injuries by close encounters with thorny bushes and rugged brush. Gloves for dirt riders are reinforced with strips of thick rubber that run along the back of fingers to the wrist.

Motocross gloves are cleaned with mild soap and water. Too much water is not good, so wash the gloves using a cloth dampened with soapy water and rinse with a clean cloth dampened with just clear water. A toothbrush is used along rubber strips to remove dirt build-up and other stubborn debris.

After cleaning, treat gloves with a light application of Lexol or other leather conditioner. Go easy on the application to the palm and front finger portion of the gloves. Too much conditioner may cause the gloves to be slippery, which will reduce grip strength. Rub in conditioner with a soft cloth, using a dry side of the cloth to buff off excess.

Optional plastic hand protectors attached to the handlebars are a great idea for dirt and desert riders. As a result of high speeds during the Baja trip, those protectors on Ralph Maughn's bike were

Motocross gloves are cleaned with a little mild soap, water and a brush. Street gloves generally come clean with just a wipe with a damp wash mitt. Either way, they are easiest to clean while wearing them. Your hand offers a solid base and also stretches the material to make it wrinkle-free.

covered with thorns that completely penetrated the plastic. You can just imagine what the back of his hands would have looked like without the protection of those plastic guards.

Street motorcycle enthusiasts wear gloves designed for comfort and warmth, as opposed to motocross gloves which are made to withstand rugged use and offer protection against harsh impacts. To achieve optimum cleaning and conditioning results for fine riding gloves, it is best to use the products and methods recommended by the individual glove manufacturer. Instructions for glove care are normally written on a tag attached to the gloves. When in doubt, consult the folks at the motorcycle shop where the gloves were purchased.

Basic glove cleaning is done with clear water and a soft cloth. There is no advantage in soaking gloves with water, rather, it is most beneficial to keep them as dry as possible. This will help to prevent mildew from forming inside and also keep the material from drying out. For extra-dirty gloves, dip the cloth in a mixture of mild soapy water and wring out excess so the cloth is damp, not dripping.

While off of your hands, gloves are difficult to clean. The material stretches and folds, making it hard to maintain a smooth surface to work on. You may have the best luck cleaning gloves while on your hands. Put a glove on one hand and use the other hand to vigorously wipe with the cloth. Use a toothbrush in seams to remove bug residue and other debris. Dry with a clean cloth. It is easy to clean all parts of the glove, especially around fingers, with the glove on your hand and stretched tight.

The back sides of gloves are most susceptible to debris and fading. Black gloves suffer the most, as rays from the sun quickly dry out the material and bleach out color. This is why it is important to keep a good coat of conditioner on gloves. Art Wentworth has always preferred soft doeskin gloves. He likes to clean them once a month, which includes a light treatment of conditioner. His gloves have remained soft and good looking for a long time, since conditioner has prevented the material from drying out and cracking.

You can purchase leather conditioners at leather stores and shoe shops, along with motorcycle shops that sell leather accessories. Follow the instructions on the label. Too much is not good, so use sparingly. Work conditioner into the material and then let it sit for a few hours, even over night. Then buff with a clean cloth.

Riding leathers

The most expensive rider accessories are leather coats and pants. Proper care of these items will extend their life span for years. Avid motorcycle riders wear leathers for warmth and comfort, as well as protection. You will never see a profes-

sional motorcycle racer compete without full leathers. The outfit may not prevent broken bones or bruises in the event of a fall, but it will protect the racer's skin against cuts and abrasions. Leathers also serve as sort of a brake when a downed rider slides on the ground. Most racers try to slide during a spill rather than roll. Rolls cause broken bones while slides generally just wear out leathers.

Cleaning

Like gloves, coats and pants are easiest to clean while you are wearing them. The material can be stretched tight with your free hand, while your body provides a solid base. Every part of the

Leather coats and pants are also easiest to clean while you are wearing them. Your body makes a perfect rack and offers a solid base. Because of this, it is most convenient to wash riding gear immediately upon return from a ride. Residue will be fresh and easy to remove, and you'll already have the gear on. Most of the time, riding leathers are cleaned with clear water and a damp wash mitt. Wring out the mitt completely, as there is no need to get the gear soaking wet. Wash the coat and pants as you would your body while showering; start at the shoulders and work down. With your free hand, hold the cuff to stretch the sleeve and pull the material tight for easy and complete cleaning.

141

After a wash mitt cleaning, use a clean towel to remove water streaks. Use the mitt again, if need be, to clean spots missed the first time.

outfit can easily be reached, except for the back of the coat. That part can be washed by a friend, or, you can drape the coat over the back of a chair. A chair holds the coat in place while your free hand stretches the material from the bottom, making the coat taut and manageable.

Most leather coats and pants have sewn-on labels that include cleaning and conditioning instructions. I recommend you follow those instructions.

Bug residue, dirt and road film should be washed off as soon as possible, before they have time to harden and impregnate the pores of leather coats and pants. Because of this, and since leathers are easiest to clean while you are wearing them, it is most convenient to clean them immediately after a ride. Not much more than a clean wash mitt and clear water is needed.

Fill a bucket with clear water and rinse the wash mitt. Wring out excess water so the mitt is damp. Wash the coat starting at the shoulders and work down, as if you were taking a shower. Stubborn residue is attacked with a soft toothbrush, along with any build-up along seams, beads and snaps. Hold the end of the sleeve with your free hand to stretch the material, making cleaning more complete.

Periodically rinse the mitt in clear water and wring out excess. Pay close attention to the front of the coat and shin areas of the pants. These are the places most apt to collect bug splatter and dirt. When the outfit is clean, use a soft towel to dry.

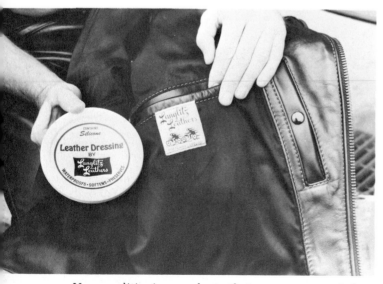

Use conditioning products that are recommended or supplied by the leather manufacturer. This assures you that the right ingredients are applied to the material to ensure longest-lasting protection and preservation.

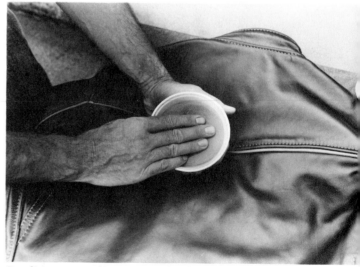

Conditioner application on leathers is most conveniently made by hand. Your fingers can smear conditioner into seams and along beads much easier and quicker than a cloth. Use seams and beads as guides and apply conditioner to just one panel at a time. This gives you a pattern to work from, which helps you maintain complete and uniform coverage.

Conditioning

You will never go wrong using a leather conditioner made specifically for the brand of leathers you own. Langlitz leathers should be treated with Langlitz Leather Conditioner, just as Alpinestars boots should be serviced with Alpinestars products. Leather conditioner adds longevity to the material by preserving it and also helps to keep it waterproof, a real bonus when you find yourself in the middle of an unexpected rainstorm. Treat leathers when they are brand new to make bug residue removal easier. Treat zippers with a silicone zipper conditioner to keep them in perfect operation.

Although leathers are most manageable to wash while you are wearing them, conditioner application is best made while leathers are laid flat on a table and fully zipped. In this position, it is easier to apply treatment deep into seams and along beads.

Work conditioner into the material with your hand. A soft cloth may be used, but many enthusiasts have found that bare hands and fingers work better. A cloth is difficult to manage, fingers can work conditioner into seams and along beads much more efficiently. Rub in conditioner a panel at a time. This will give you a pattern to follow which will ensure complete coverage.

The coat's front side requires conditioner as a waterproofing agent and as a preventative measure to keep debris from impregnating the material. The back side and shoulders are vulnerable to fading and drying as a result of continuous exposure to the sun, therefore needing conditioner treatment as much as the front.

Conditioner should be applied to pants, along with the coat, to provide the same degree of material protection and waterproofing. Close attention should be paid to the shin areas because they are most likely to be bombarded by road hazards. Seams at the crotch are just as important, but for a different reason. Anyone who has ridden in the rain knows that the crotch is one of the first places to get wet. Wetness at the crotch, combined with the wind-chill factor, makes for a very miserable and uncomfortable ride. Be sure seams in that area receive an adequate amount of conditioner.

Upon completion of conditioner application, hang leathers on sturdy coat hangers and suspend them in a warm, dry place. Allow conditioner to soak in for a few hours; overnight is not too long. After that, use a soft cloth to buff leathers and remove excess conditioner.

Treating leathers with conditioner should be done at least twice a year, and subsequent applications made as the outfit becomes dry or dull looking. You be the judge. If your leathers are looking tacky or starting to lose their waterproof effectiveness, wash them off and apply a light coat of condi-

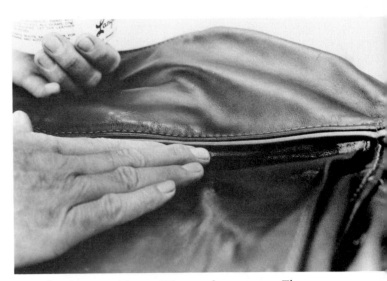

Don't be skimpy with conditioner along seams. These are the spots most likely to leak water when you're caught in a rainstorm.

tioner. It is better to perform this task too often as opposed to not often enough.

Boots

Quality motorcycle boots, like leathers, are expensive. Cleaning and preserving them is just as important as leather care, and the procedure for their service employs the same basic technique. Boots are serviced twice a year and anytime they begin to leak, dry out or look dull and tacky.

Boot shops sell a variety of conditioners and waterproofing agents. If you cannot find a specific

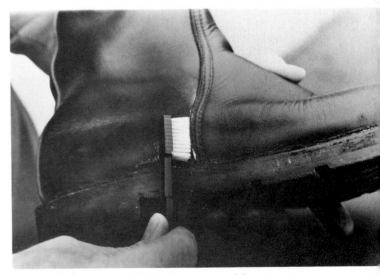

Mud and debris caught in the seams of boots are removed with a soft toothbrush. A little clear water on the brush helps to loosen stubborn debris.

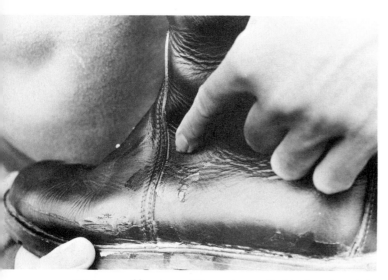

Waterproof boot conditioner is applied by hand, as it is on leather coats and pants. Apply a good bead of waterproof boot conditioner along the sole seam. Excess is removed later, after it has had plenty of time to soak in. The same kind of bead is applied to stitching and seams as is along the sole. Be sure to completely cover the threaded stitches to protect them from water absorption.

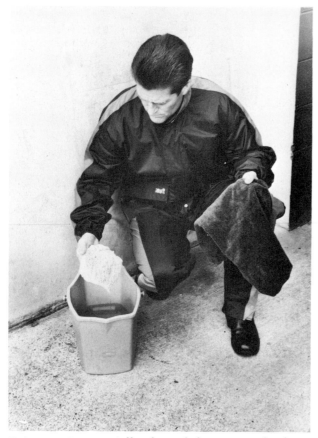

Rain gear is essentially cleaned the same as leathers. Most of the time, all you need is a wash mitt and clear water. Have a towel at hand for drying.

product recommended for the brand of boots you wear, seek advice from a boot shop salesperson.

A wash mitt and clear water is generally all that is needed for boot cleaning. Motocross boots may require a mild soapy solution, a toothbrush and more water than street boots because of the amount of dirt and mud that usually gets on them. While on your feet, use the mitt to wipe off dust and dirt. Use a toothbrush to dislodge debris in seams and along the bead between the sole and boot body.

Wally Shearer's boots get pretty dirty on the motocross track. At the end of the day, he uses a stout brush to knock off all the big chunks of mud. Then, he lets the boots dry for a day or two. At that point, he uses a smaller brush to completely remove caked-on mud, dirt, sand and other debris. When they are clean, he applies a liberal coat of Uncle Herbert's Boot Grease to keep the leather pliable and waterproof.

Alpinestars Waterproof Shoe Paste includes silicones and bee's wax. The ingredients make boots look good but more importantly serve as a waterproofing agent. This is important for riders who like to take long trips and don't care about periodic rain showers, and those who depend on their motorcycle as a sole source of transportation and must ride in any kind of weather.

Apply conditioner with your hand. Don't be skimpy on seams and stitching or the bead around the sole. These are the places most likely to leak when subjected to rain and water thrown up by the front tire. To ensure that a good film is put into seams, use your finger to lay a bead of conditioner along them. Then, work conditioner into the seams until you see that coverage is complete.

Upon completion of conditioner application, set boots in a dry, warm place. A windowsill in the sunlight is perfect. Let them stand for a couple of hours to allow silicones to settle into the boot material before buffing with a clean cloth.

Rain gear

Lightweight nylon rain gear neatly fits into fanny packs, tank packs and saddlebags. Since it doesn't take up much room, pleasure riders should have it at the ready, especially on extended day or weekend trips. Heavier, rubber-type rain gear may be more suitable for the everyday rider who expects wet weather on a frequent basis.

Weatherproof rain gear should be washed immediately at the conclusion of a wet ride to prevent dirt and road film from setting up. Because washing this gear is easiest with it on, it is most convenient to do this at the end of a ride while you are still wearing it. Clear water and a wash mitt is usually all that is needed. However, on occasion, you may need to use a mild soapy solution and a toothbrush to wash rain gear subjected to extra-dirty conditions, and to remove grit and grime caught in seams. Always be sure to check the label attached to rain gear for specific washing and drying instructions.

With the rain suit on, start washing at the shoulders and work down with a damp wash mitt. Bug residue will come off with water, although it may take a few swipes and some vigorous rubbing with the mitt. Wash the front of leg panels twice, since they receive the bulk of dirt and grime splashed from the road. Dry the suit with a clean towel.

For severely soiled rain gear, fill a tub, sink or pail with clear water and dunk the gear for intensive cleaning. Don't scrub the material, just rub it with the wash mitt to remove dirt and road water grime.

Hang the clean suit in a place where it can drip dry, like a shower stall or bathtub. After a few

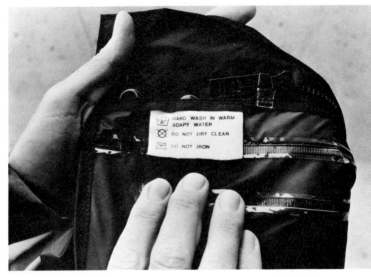

Cleaning instructions usually accompany rain gear. Follow these directions to ensure the best care is given your gear so that it performs as expected time after time.

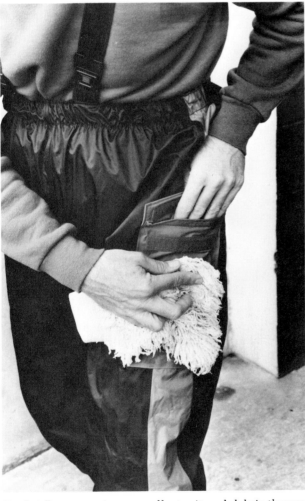

Pocket flaps on rain gear collect grit and debris thrown up by the front tire during wet weather riding. Be sure to open flaps and clean under them. You should check the condition of pockets, too.

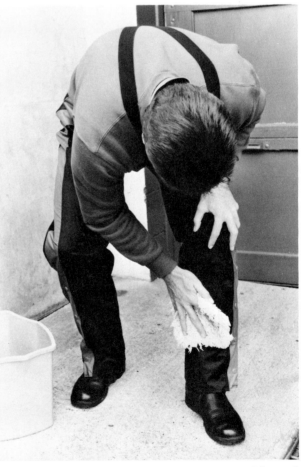

Shin areas on riding gear suffer the most road hazard abuse. They are constantly bombarded by debris thrown up by the front tire. Wash these areas a couple of times to be sure all road film is washed away.

145

hours, turn the suit inside out so the inside can dry. Hanging from a coat hanger, interior panels will not dry nearly as fast as the outside, so always be certain the entire rain suit is totally dry before stowing in a pack or saddlebag. Residual water left on a stored rain suit could mildew, making it rather unpleasant or impossible to wear the next time you find yourself in wet riding conditions.

Use a clean soft towel to dry riding gear. Since this equipment is usually stowed away in a fanny pack or saddlebag, you must be sure all moisture is gone to prevent the formation of mildew.

Chapter 12

Road trips and storage

Preparation for road trips is varied, depending on the distance to be traveled, the route to be taken and the amount of time one expects to be gone. Touring motorcycle enthusiasts generally plan for extended trips, which justify the need for large saddlebags and tour-paks to carry their assortment of clothes, camping gear and recreational equipment. Sport bike riders usually opt for one- or two-day excursions and can get by with fanny and tank packs.

Numerous motorcycle magazines have published an array of articles about motorcycle travel, and most modern libraries stock a considerable number of those magazines. It doesn't take long to search through the magazine microfiche at the library to find specific articles about motorcycle

Sport bikes are designed more for actual riding pleasure than for comfortable long-distance traveling. Detailing before a trip assures the rider that an adequate amount of wax is on painted pieces and that service checks have been performed.

Engine detailing gives you an opportunity to go over the motor with a fine-tooth comb. Loose nuts and bolts should be torqued, frayed wires repaired and cracked hoses replaced—before they cause a breakdown on your trip.

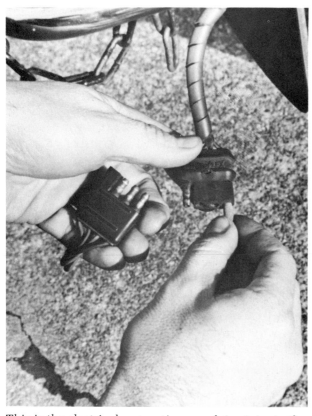

This is the electrical connection supplying juice to the trailer lights on Don Perry's trailer. Corrosion on the male prongs and inside the female receptacles caused a shortage of electricity to the trailer lights, making them exceptionally dim. Perry used #600 wet-and-dry sandpaper to clean the male ends and rolled it up tightly to fit inside the female plug for cleaning.

touring. Reading these articles and talking to other enthusiasts about their touring experiences will help you to have a safe, pleasant and well-planned journey.

Detailing before traveling

Since motorcycles get so dirty on road trips, many feel it is easier to quickly wash their bike before the trip and save extensive detailing for trip's end. Although detailing before and after the trip may seem redundant, it is the best way to protect your bike. In essence, the pre-trip detail may even make post-trip detailing easier.

Don't forget that detailing is not limited to cleaning. It also includes waxing and protection measures designed to prolong the life of motorcycle parts and accessories. Wax on the front fender, for example, will help to prevent road grime from becoming embedded in paint. Conditioning leathers before the trip will help to repel ultraviolet sun rays, adding protection against premature fading, drying and cracking. And, wax on your helmet adds needed protection against bug splatter and paint chips.

Detailing allows you the opportunity to go over your motorcycle with a fine-tooth comb. You will have the chance to check nuts and bolts for tightness, cables and tires for wear, forks and differential for fluid level, chain for proper adjustment and almost every other part of the bike as necessary.

Don Perry has put a lot of miles on his 1980 Honda Gold Wing Interstate. The bike not only looks good, but has also performed as expected, trip after trip. Perry attributes this dependability to conscientious maintenance.

He changes the radiator fluid once a year using a 50/50 mix of antifreeze and distilled water. He prefers distilled water because of its purity, and has outstanding results. Oil is changed every 3,000 miles using Golden Spectro 4, a synthetic/petroleum lubricant. Although this engine oil is expensive at $4.95 a quart, Perry says it works like magic to keep gear shifting extra quiet and smooth. He also changes fluid in the drive shaft differential with each engine oil change. Fork fluid is drained and refilled as per Honda's recommendations.

During a road trip, Perry was pulled over by a police officer. He was puzzled by this because he was not speeding and had not seen a traffic light or stop sign for a hundred miles. As it turned out, the officer pulled him over because the taillights on his motorcycle trailer were dimly lit, almost to the point of being invisible.

The problem was confusing because instruments showed a full charge going through the electrical system with no unusual draws, and, the headlight was burning brightly. To make a long story short, the problem was traced to the electrical connection between the trailer and the motorcycle.

The male and female ends of the plug had corroded just enough to make contact minimal, causing an inadequate amount of electricity to flow through to the trailer lights. A quick cleaning with #600 sandpaper solved the problem and allowed the taillights to shine with normal intensity. Needless to say, this has become a regular item in Perry's detailing and maintenance schedule.

Nothing can spoil a motorcycle trip faster than a breakdown. It is extremely frustrating to have to push a bike twenty or thirty miles to a gas station in hopes that there is a mechanic on duty who understands motorcycles. It is even worse if you have a big bike requiring the use of a tow truck. Be on the safe side and follow the maintenance schedule provided in the owners handbook. On long trips, carry spare parts such as spark plugs, cables and master links.

Bill Buckingham fills the tires on his bike to maximum pressure before starting out on a trip during hot weather. High air pressure keeps tires tight and rigid. Maintaining recommended air pressure reduces tire flexibility. As tires flex, friction generates heat which increases wear.

Ralph Maughn is a stickler for maintenance. He realized the excessive amount of dust his motorcycle was being subjected to during the Baja trip, and the extra importance of maintaining a good seal around the air filter and housing. But unfortunately, he failed to bring along a tube of petroleum jelly or other suitable sealant. Since he is a seasoned motorcycle riding veteran of some twenty-five years, he did, however, carry an ample supply of Preparation-H. It performed well (as directed) and also as a good air cleaner gasket sealer.

Motorcycle guys are always on their toes, aren't they?

Along with detailing for appearance, you should always take pains to maintain the performance features of your bike. Make sure the brake and clutch fluid reservoirs are filled to prescribed levels. Take care of the chain and lubricate it when conditions warrant. The same is true for radiators, engines and air pressures. In a few words, expect the unexpected, prepare for the worst, be ready for those trivial breakdowns, and enjoy your road trip as much as anticipated.

Parts storage

I doubt the spare parts and bare bones storage of Ralph Maughn's Baja trip compare to Don Perry's road touring needs. Maughn planned 2,100 miles of high-speed desert riding while Perry's plans usually include smooth highways and frequent rest stops. Maughn knew he would be out in the middle of nowhere, while Perry follows frequently traveled routes in close proximity to cities and towns where broken parts could be easily replaced.

Maughn placed a couple of dozen strips of duct tape on the lower forks of his Yamaha, each about a foot long. This relieved him of having to stow an entire roll of tape somewhere else. Over the tape, he covered the lower forks with hose clamps. During the trip, tape and clamps were used to hold the rear fender when one of its mounts gave way.

Ingenious spare part storage may include taping spare cables to existing ones, securing extra hand levers to the handlebars and carrying new

During the extensive pre-trip detail and service of his Yamaha, Ralph Maughn took time to grease axles and all other parts requiring that service. Sandpaper, in this picture, was used to remove the slight glazing on brake shoes.

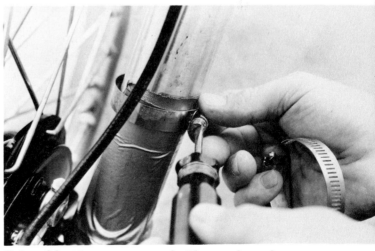

Strips of duct tape were covered with water hose clamps on the front forks of Dave Ireland's and Ralph Maughn's bikes in preparation for the Baja trip. Storage at this location did not compromise maneuverability of the bike, and the parts didn't take up room in crowded backpacks.

master links in the tool kit. From past experience, recognize which parts have given you trouble and be sure extra ones are taken on the trip.

Large plastic trash bags tightly folded take up very little room in a saddlebag or tank pack. Motorcycle enthusiasts have used them as rain gear when unexpectedly caught in wet weather. They punch holes in the bag for their head and arms and wear it like a poncho. Additional bags are used for their legs. Rory Vance places clean clothes inside plastic bags before stowing them in the saddlebags of his Katana. This gives him added assurance that his clothes will be clean and dry should the saddlebags leak water or accumulate dust.

Art Wentworth buys woven belts with slip-through tension buckles at the surplus store, like those worn by Navy personnel. He winds them up in a tight roll and secures with a rubber band. They do not take up much room and can be used to lash down tote bags and other items on the bike. The belts are soft and will not scratch frame members or other points of attachment.

A number of smaller items can be brought along on road trips to make the ride enjoyable. Of most importance though, is a tool kit. Most motorcycles are equipped with handy tool kits from the factory. They include spark plug sockets, pliers, screwdrivers and assorted wrenches. Add to the kit as necessary to be sure you have the means to tighten nuts and bolts, adjust the chain and cables, change fouled spark plugs, insert new fuses and clean electrical connections.

Dave Ireland has a motorcycle just like Ralph Maughn's. He made the Baja trip with Maughn, along with a couple of other riders. Months before the trip, they frequently got together to make definitive travel plans. Of utmost importance were the tools and mechanical equipment they thought may be needed along the way.

Instead of carrying a bulky tent, they brought a lightweight nylon tarp. As a makeshift tent, it was secured to the motorcycles which were parked in a circle. Besides spare cables and chain lube, they carried a patch kit for the inner tube, spare inner tubes, valve stem tools, air pump, feeler gauges for valve and plug adjustment, liquid weld, oil, carburetor cleaner and tire wrenches. Because of the heat, they changed the oil in their bikes five times.

Trips like these require riders to be well prepared. You should read as many magazine articles as you can about this type of travel, and talk to fellow motorcycle enthusiasts who have experience in the field.

Detailing supplies

Don Perry might be able to squeeze a wash bucket, mitt and towels into his trailer, but Rory Vance would have a tough time fitting all of that into his saddlebags. The need to clean a motorcycle while on an extended trip is debatable. A quick cleaning of the windshield and lights is probably more in line with customary riding.

Mike Johnson made an extended tour on his 1986 Harley-Davidson Low Glide. During a leg of the trip in a farmland area, he found himself driving through a blizzard of grasshoppers. It didn't last long, but his bike was totally covered with grasshopper residue, especially the engine.

When he finally got to a town, Johnson located a self-serve car wash. Because he had always kept the bike detailed and protected with a good coat of quality wax, the intensive rinse at the car wash was all that was needed to get his bike sparkling clean again. Without a coat of wax, grasshopper residue would have been much more difficult to remove.

In a city or town, you can always stop at a gas station to use wet paper towels for removing bug splatter on windshields. You can also retrieve napkins from a restaurant to remove windshield debris. But in the middle of the mountains or desert, you may have a problem locating paper towels or water. For this reason, you might consider filling a small container with plastic polish and include with it a tight wad of napkins or paper towels. Use them in isolated areas to remove debris from windshields, lights and helmets.

A towel should also be considered a handy detailing item to take along on trips. Many times, parking overnight will result in dew settling on

Tool kits are heaven-sent in time of need, especially when you break down on a long trip, many miles from your tool box. During the pre-trip detail, and at least once a month, check the condition of tools and make sure they function properly. WD-40 works well as a lubricant and provides a light film which acts as somewhat of a rust inhibitor.

seats, windshield and handgrips. A medium-size bath towel is ideal for drying these parts and others as you see fit.

Road oil and other petroleum-based debris are easiest to remove the sooner cleaning takes place. These substances harden over time and will require polish for their removal if left in place too long. Art Wentworth has carried a small container of Meguiar's Car Cleaner Wax and a small towel on road trips. On occasion, he has used it to remove road oil and tar at the end of a day's ride. One-step cleaner wax removes debris and also offers wax protection in one quick application. Not only will this maneuver make the bike look better for the rest of the trip, but it will also make the end of the trip detail that much easier.

Motorcycle storage

Motorcycles are frequently stored indoors during harsh winter months. Allowing a dirty bike to sit idle for months is not good. Dirt accumulations absorb moisture and give rust and corrosion a starting place. Painted parts lacking wax protection are subject to oxidation. And dry chains will stiffen and may rust if confronted with moisture.

Thus, before storage, a motorcycle should be detailed, fully serviced and placed under a quality cotton cover that breathes.

Squire Tomasie and Bill Buckingham always wash motorcycles cold. They also recommend that bikes be ridden after washing to help blow off water from the engine and dry moisture that may have settled in exhaust pipes. This is especially important before parking a motorcycle for extended storage.

Washing a motorcycle that is still hot from operation creates steam, which may find its way into the cylinders. If the moisture is allowed to stay there, cylinder walls will start to rust. The same problem exists when a cold motorcycle is washed and then left wet and idle for long periods. Moisture in the exhaust pipes will evaporate and eventually creep through open valves to begin a rusting process on bare cylinder walls. Rust problems also exist for exterior parts left wet during storage.

After a short ride, use a soft clean towel to absorb lingering water spots and remove dust that may have gotten on the bike. Let the engine cool down, turn off the fuel and disconnect the battery before installing the motorcycle cover. Be sure the

Art Wentworth likes to carry along a small vial of plastic polish on road trips to the mountains. He uses it to wipe off encrusted bug leftovers from the windshield and helmet face shield.

A quality cotton motorcycle cover from Beverly Hills Motoring Accessories covers Squire Tomasie's brand-new Kawasaki ZX-10. Plastic covers and those that are airtight are not recommended, as moisture is trapped inside and surrounds the bike. Most enthusiasts prefer cotton covers that breathe.

tires are covered too. Prolonged exposure to the sun, by way of a window or skylight, will dry out rubber tires and may cause sidewalls to crack or split.

Enthusiasts disagree on the application of vinyl dressing just before storage. Some feel that dressing adds protection during storage, while others believe the added moisture attracts more moisture to cause mildew. A very light application of dressing, with all excess buffed out, may be good. On the other hand, vinyl and rubber parts that are clean and dry should remain in good shape as long as they are protected from moisture and sunlight by way of a quality cover.

It is a good idea to start motorcycles periodically during storage. This allows cylinder walls to be coated with oil and disperses any tiny pockets of water that may have formed inside the engine, and will also help to recharge the battery. Operate the engine for about fifteen minutes or until it heats up to operating temperature. Once a month is not too often.

All parts of the motorcycle should be checked out when the bike is brought out of storage. Visually inspect it for obvious problems such as flat tires, cracked hoses, low fluid levels and dry chain. When the bike is first started, allow it to run at low rpm so that the cylinder walls can be coated with oil. Operate all the lights, levers and foot pedals. Start the ride slowly and be cautious of sticky brakes, especially drum brakes. Moisture may have settled on brake shoes, causing some corrosion which might make them a bit sticky for the first few stops. Take care of any mechanical problems immediately to ensure a safe ride and an enjoyable riding season.

Chapter 13

Overview

A complete motorcycle detail is labor intensive and time consuming. This endeavor is made easier by maintaining your motorcycle on a regular weekly schedule, or after every ride. Thorough washing does not take a great deal of time on a relatively clean bike. Attention given to specific areas with each wash will ensure complete coverage on a monthly basis.

For example, if you wash your motorcycle once a week, divide the bike into four parts. Something like, wheels and tires; painted parts; chrome, rubber and vinyl; and accessories. On the first week, along with the wash, polish and wax the wheels and dress the tires. The second week, polish (as needed) and wax all painted parts. After washing on the third week, shine chrome and dress

Motorcycles are busy and intricate machines. Comprehensive detailing takes a lot of time and labor. Frequent washing, polishing and waxing help to keep the bike in

good shape and make the annual or semi-annual detail less of a labor-intensive endeavor.

Regular washing should be patterned after the initial detail wash. Use paintbrushes and toothbrushes as necessary to remove dirt build-up and stubborn bug residue.

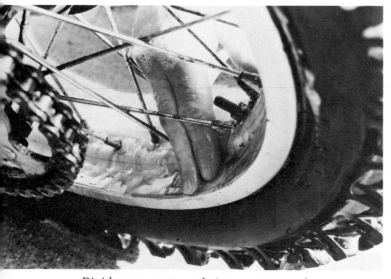

Divide your motorcycle into sections and give extra attention to a particular section every week along with the wash. Wheels and tires may be classified as one section, and you can spend extra time cleaning and shining them one week a month after the wash.

On the second week, pay extra attention to all painted parts. Polish as needed and then wax. Inspect each piece for wax build-up and remove with a toothbrush or cut-off paintbrush.

154

selected rubber and vinyl parts. Finally, on the fourth week, spend extra time cleaning and servicing accessories like saddlebags, cables, chain, windshield and so forth.

Performing this type of regular maintenance will keep your motorcycle looking good and give you the opportunity to check for loose nuts and bolts, frayed wires and cables, paint chips, tire wear and so on. In short time, you will develop a pattern for washing and servicing your motorcycle; it will become a routine. When that happens, you will find yourself completing the job faster with hardly any wasted effort.

Clean motorcycle spiff

Many times, a motorcycle will only be dusty. It needs to be cleaned, but the amount of dust and lint does not warrant a full-blown wash and wax. For those jobs, Dan Mycon uses glass cleaner and a soft towel to wipe off the bike.

At Bellevue Suzuki, Vince Barbeaux likes to keep the bikes looking bright and shiny on the showroom floor. He uses a product called Klean 'n Shine to buff off fingerprints and remove dust. Gina Buckingham uses Protect All to dust and shine the new BMWs at Buckingham BMW in Seattle, with excellent results.

If your bike has been sitting in the garage for a while and has gathered a thin layer of dust, consider using a glass cleaner or other mild cleaner to brighten it up. Of course, the bike had to be clean to begin with, as this kind of mild dusting will not remove baked-on dirt and grime.

Washing

Most of your washing supplies are carried in the wash bucket. One of the most useful motorcycle cleaning tools, besides the wash mitt, is a soft floppy paintbrush. Always carry it along with the wash mitt and bucket. After soaping up a section with the mitt, use the paintbrush to quickly clean tight spots and in grooves and along seams. You should also carry a scrub brush for tires and foot rubbers, an SOS pad for stubborn spots, a toothbrush for tight spots and a spray bottle of Simple Green, S100 or other suitable cleaner.

Start the wash at the bottom of the bike while the ground is still dry. Spray cleaner liberally and allow it to soak in for about a minute. Then wash with an old wash mitt. Rinse with plenty of water and move on, just like the initial wash before a detail.

Move around the bike in a systematic manner and be sure to wash everything; don't leave an area until it is clean. Use all the tools at your disposal and retrieve additional tools as necessary, such as a can of Gunk or solvent, paper towel or rag.

When the bike has been completely washed, use a soft towel to dry it as much as possible. Then,

The third week may be dedicated to chrome, vinyl and rubber. Use allotted time to polish and wax chrome pieces such as these on an Electra Glide. Dress weathered vinyl and rubber pieces and be sure to buff off all excess.

After washing on the fourth week, closely examine saddlebags and other accessories. Touch up paint chips, polish and wax as you see fit. You should also check the chain for lubrication, as well as cables and linkages.

155

take it for a quick spin up the street. If the weather is bad or the streets are wet or dusty, just start the engine and let it idle up to operating temperature or until all water has been evaporated from the engine and exhaust pipes. Use a damp towel to wipe off dust or dirt that has accumulated on the fairing or wheels during the dry-off ride.

Your motorcycle should be looking pretty good at this point. According to your schedule, perform extras at this time. If you had planned to polish and wax the exhaust pipes, let them cool off before starting. Before waxing painted parts, remove any water droplets, as they will hinder the process. Remove spots of chain lube from the rear wheel before polishing or waxing.

Mechanical service work

Jobs such as changing the oil and adjusting chains and cables are made more pleasant when the motorcycle is clean. While oil is draining from

the engine and drive shaft differential, you can check the tightness of nuts and bolts all over the motorcycle. Check the battery for water level and inspect other reservoirs for fluid levels. Follow the

Vince Barbeaux sells motorcycles at Bellevue Suzuki in Bellevue, Washington. Bikes in the showroom get dusty and suffer handprints from curious customers. Instead of subjecting the bikes to constant washing, he uses an all-purpose household polish to dust and shine them. Klean 'n Shine polish is applied to the fuel tank on a Suzuki. Barbeaux wipes it on with a soft cloth and buffs the paint to perfection. He says this product is great for removing dust and fingerprints from paint, chrome and vinyl.

Vehicles that have been sitting idle for a while may simply be dusty. Use a soft cloth and dry paintbrush to remove accumulations of dust and at the same time check for frayed cables and wires, incipient rust spots on chrome and any other items of concern.

Gina Buckingham keeps the bikes in the showroom looking good at her dad's (Bill Buckingham) BMW shop in Seattle, Washington. She uses a product called Protect All to clean and shine dusty bikes, with excellent results.

manufacturer's recommendations for product usage, lubrication frequency and adjustment specifications.

The best guide to follow for normal maintenance checks is the owners manual that came with your motorcycle. If you bought a used bike with no manual and are unfamiliar with maintenance procedures, check with the folks at the local motorcycle shop. I have found most of these people quite friendly and eager to talk about anything that has to do with motorcycles, whether it be of a mechanical nature or about actual motorcycle riding. Every motorcycle shop employee I have met or talked to owns a motorcycle and is an avid motorcycle enthusiast.

Wally Shearer cleans the chain on his motocross bike with a wire brush and sprays it with WD-40 at the end of every moto. When he takes a bike out for pleasure riding in the dirt, a different lube is used. Riding on wet terrain and on extended trips requires a thick lubricant that won't easily wash or wear off. Consider the type of riding you expect to do and find out from experienced motorcycle mechanics which is the best product for the chain on your motorcycle.

Rider accessories

Riding boots and leathers are expensive items that should be taken care of. It may not be necessary to condition them more than twice a year, but, cleaning should take place after every ride. All you'll need is a bucket of clear water and a clean cotton wash mitt. While still wearing the outfit, use the damp mitt to wipe off dust and remove bug residue. Dry it off with a clean towel.

Helmets should be given the same attention. If you encountered a blemish or scratch on the face shield, use plastic polish to buff it away. Apply Rain-X or other water-shedding product as you deem necessary.

Tank bags and fanny packs are wiped off with a damp mitt, dried and removed for storage. It is a good idea to check inside the packs, especially after an extended trip. You may have left something in them that needs to be taken out, like food or other perishables. Take a quick look at the straps to make sure they are not frayed or worn, and check that part of the bike where packs were secured. Sometimes bags are secured incorrectly and cause paint damage. Scratches should be polished out and then waxed, and paint chips should be touched up.

Final overview

This book is filled with advice on how to make your motorcycle look its best. Enthusiasts disagree on product usage, but overwhelmingly concur that the mildest cleaning and polishing techniques are safest and most preferred. They recognize the

All-purpose household polish will not clean a filthy motorcycle. If your weekly wash confronts you with a bike in this condition, you'll need the strength of Simple Green or a comparable cleaner to remove road film and grime.

quick-cleaning ability of harsh chemicals and abrasives, but cringe at the thought of applying them to a pristine motorcycle. Rather, they may accept the use of these harsh methods once, on a used motorcycle that has been sorely neglected. After that,

Once or twice a month for dirt bikes, less often for road machines, disassemble and remove the throttle grip for cleaning and lubrication. Wally Shearer does this after every motocross race and is convinced that is why he has never had this part break on his bike. After cleaning, use the recommended lubricant and be sure you put the piece back together correctly. Screws that secure the throttle grip are to be tightened equally. If not, the grip will be sticky and not operate as smoothly as it is supposed to.

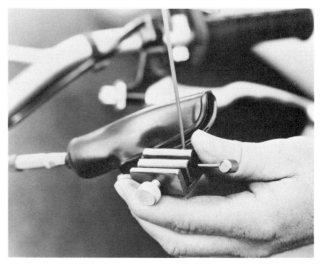

At least as often as recommended by the manufacturer, lubricate linkages and all moving parts on the bike. Heavy washing can remove some degree of lubrication from various parts. Dirt bikes are most susceptible to inadequate lubrication, and special attention to this maintenance tip is recommended.

This is a cable luber, which is used by many motorcycle enthusiasts and mechanics to completely and thoroughly lube cables. It is secured to the cable end by a set screw. Lubricant is sprayed into a hole in the top of it and is forced into the cable. When you notice lube coming out of the other end of the cable, you are assured that lube has passed through all of it.

If your bike is not equipped with a center stand, use a makeshift support to hold the bike while you slowly spin the back wheel to apply chain lube. Here, Wally Shearer is using Yamaha Lube-Zall to service the chain on a YZ 80.

mild methods and products are their means with which to keep a motorcycle standing tall.

Dan Mycon says it is a shame that a two- or three-day motorcycle detail can be ruined by just a five-minute ride. This may be true because bikes are so open and susceptible to dirt and road hazards. But, we have all seen bikes that have never been detailed and seldom, if ever, washed. Who would want to ride such an eyesore?

Motorcycles are unique machines and enthusiasts take special pride in their rides. I think you will find that even non-enthusiasts will turn their heads to look at a motorcycle that looks clean, crisp and sparkling. More than just transportation, motorcycles are a fun means of getting from one place to another, an expression of freedom and an enjoyable form of travel that has to be experienced to be appreciated.

Lots of people refuse to ride motorcycles. Some don't like the wind in their face and others get too cold. The major factor, though, is safety. All too often, we hear of a motorcyclist who has been critically injured in an accident. It is obvious that a bike affords the rider no protection from collisions with other vehicles. This is as true in the dirt as it is on the road.

Therefore, not only should you wear the right kind of riding equipment like gloves, boots, leathers and helmet, but also you must always drive defensively. As a motorcycle rider and enthusiast, I try to pay attention to motorcycle riders while I am driving a car. But, there have been occasions when I have pulled out in front of a bike only because I didn't see it. Unfortunately, many other automobile drivers have, and will continue to experience the same dilemma. Leaving the headlight on at all times will help, but you have to be aware that sometimes, you and your motorcycle are just not easily recognized.

Finally, this book is not intended to be the last word on motorcycle detailing. Rather, it is a collection of tips and recommendations that work for some avid motorcycle enthusiasts. Everyone has their preferred methods and techniques. If you have a favorite way of taking care of your bike that works well and lasts long, why change? The bottom line is a clean motorcycle that stands tall, looks crisp and sparkles like a show machine.

I hope that you continue to enjoy a lifetime of safe motorcycle riding, and that the information in this book has helped you to achieve the ultimate motorcycle detail.

Bug residue to the right of the wash mitt is easily removed with the mitt and clear water. Cleaning leathers after every ride is recommended, and it is easiest to remove residue while it is fresh, and easiest to clean leath- *ers while you are wearing them. This will ensure that the riding gear is clean and ready to go the next time you want to hop on your bike and go for a ride.*

Index